RECYCLOPEDIA

Games, Science Equipment, and Crafts from Recycled Materials

Written and illustrated by

ROBIN SIMONS

Developed at the Boston Children's Museum

Houghton Mifflin Company Boston

For Lennie

Thank you to: Cathy Corum, Becky Corwin, Jan Goodman,
Liz Hastie, Jane Klein, Dottie Merrill, Gingy McClung, Susan
Porter, Geri Robinson, Bernie Zubrowski, and the rest of the
Children's Museum Staff for all those meetings on the staircase
where we shared ideas and learned from each other.

Library of Congress Cataloging in Publication Data

Simons, Robin.
    Recyclopedia: games, science equipment, and crafts
from recycled materials.

    SUMMARY: Suggestions for games, crafts, and scientific
equipment that can be made from recycled materials.
    1. Handicraft—Juvenile literature.   2. Games—
Juvenile literature.   3. Scientific apparatus and
instruments—Juvenile literature.   4. Recycling (waste,
etc.)—Juvenile literature.   [1. Games.   2. Scientific
apparatus and instruments.   3. Handicraft.   4. Recycling
(Waste)]   I. Title.
TT160.S46   745.5   76-17132

ISBN 0-395-24390-4
ISBN 0-395-24380-7 Paperbound Edition
Copyright © 1976 by The Children's Museum
Printed in the United States of America.
v 10 9 8 7 6 5 4

CONTENTS

CRAFTS

Introduction

To inveterate pack rats, incorrigible scroungers and habitués of the Recycle Center of the Boston Children's Museum, this book will come as no surprise. You've spotted the potential in discarded shoe boxes, old clock parts, and other "useless" objects and know that they are merely awaiting reincarnation by a pair of creative hands. To those of you who unblinkingly drop your orange juice cans in the garbage pail, don't miss the days of shirt cardboard from the cleaners, and think that factories couldn't possibly throw away anything moderately useful much less exciting and suggestive, this book will be an eye-opener. It will show you how to see those old materials in new ways and how to put them together to make the new ways work.

This is the philosophy of "Recycle." For several years a tight economy and small budgets have forced resourceful artists and teachers to look in unlikely places for inexpensive materials. The back doors of stores became a prime source for linoleum tiles, poster board, and carpet scraps that retailers throw away, and in 1971 Elaine Gurian at the Institute of Contemporary Art in Boston conceived the idea of creating a central warehouse where retail scrap materials could be collected and made easily available to large numbers of people. With backing from the Institute she designed a space and hired Leonard Gottlieb as a part-time scrounge to collect materials. Lenny, with a true scrounger's instinct (and an inside knowledge of factories), suspected that they, too, might be a source of useful scrap. In an old red station wagon and a map in his pocket, he visited local factories explaining the program and collecting materials. His suspicion proved well founded. His search uncovered the fact that factories throw away tons of potentially, if not immediately, usable materials daily, ranging from leather scraps to drinking straws to camera lenses. With the opening of the "Recycle Museum" in June, 1971, people could come and for a small fee buy a bagful of Styrofoam chips, shoe buckles, old Navy maps, or other assorted industrial discards that the Center had collected. In addition to individual bagfuls of materials, memberships were offered to those who wanted to buy large quantities of materials regularly.

The Center was well received. Gradually the number of customers—and the number of contributing industries—grew. Six months later, in January, 1972, Recycle moved to the Children's Museum. There, its space and staff were doubled, and Lenny began scrounging full-time. Withe the added drawing card of the Children's Museum and the Museum's Teacher Resource Center, the visibility of Recycle was increased. Workshops and idea sheets were added to the program. Trading was encouraged (free materials for the name of a usable source) in order to acquire new materials, and publicity was done to attract new customers. Now in its fifth year, Recycle is a highly successful, self-supporting department of the Museum, visited by thousands of people monthly.

Although storage of all the materials currently in stock (an estimated four or five tons at one time) takes most of the basement of the Resource Center building, the actual public space is one large room. Here, smaller quantities of the stock are housed in recycled bins of various kinds: old barrels, discarded cardboard tubes from paper rolls, old wooden tea crates. Shoppers finger their way from bin to bin, filling their bags, with much the feeling of an old-fashioned candy store. The bins are still fed daily by Lenny's efforts as Recycle's director.

Fifteen to twenty factories provide the core of Recycle's stock, making regular bi-weekly or monthly "donations." Another ten give materials sporadically. Many others offer occasional or one-time contributions. The materials being discarded are rejected products that don't meet a factory's quality control standards—improperly labeled ice-cream containers, not perfectly round foam-rubber balls and slightly irregularly shaped dice—or scrap material that is left over after a product is made—leather scraps from clothing manufacturers, Masonite punch-outs from stereo speakers and cardboard cards cut from pie boxes with cellophane windows—or "over-run" products that a factory has made too much of and can't sell. Often these items sit in a factory for years before being discarded. Word of such caches has brought Recycle thirty-year-old art deco can labels, 1950's pointy-toed, high-heeled wooden shoe lasts (in a variety of sizes) and outdated advertising billboards.

Despite the fact that these materials are scheduled to be discarded, factories are not always willing to see us cart them away. Donating materials to Recycle means packaging the scrap, putting it aside where it may take up valuable space, and meeting Lenny and helping him load our wagon. To many factories, hiring a disposal service to haul away all their scrap at once is a simpler, and therefore cheaper, process. Initially, for every ten factories Lenny contacted, approximately one would agree to donate. (This number has now increased as he has learned which factories are likely to donate and has become more discriminating in his contacts. To a great extent, the success of Recycle has been due to Lenny's ability to develop a reliable core of factories whose waste products are interesting to children and adults and whose administrators are open-minded and willing to cooperate in an unusual new idea.

As Recycle grew and more and more people came in to buy materials, a common refrain was heard: "This is great stuff . . . but what do you do with it?" People needed concrete, practical suggestions of ways to use the materials. This gave rise to two new dimensions of the program: workshops and idea sheets. At first geared primarily toward teachers (who formed the largest audience at Recycle) weekly workshops were offered on various uses for recycled materials in the classroom. These ranged from math and language games to arts and crafts activities and were all geared to elementary levels. Along with the workshops, we wrote up and sold printed sheets of ideas for using the materials. These functions, too, have grown, with the number and range of ideas continually expanding and the attendance at workshops soaring to standing-room-only crowds. In 1975 we expanded the format to include Saturday morning workshops for parents and children.

The philosophy of the workshops has always been to encourage people to make their own creative decisions in working with the materials. Whether a teacher making a math game or a child fashioning a toy truck, the maker will learn more in solving the technical and creative problems him- or herself than in copying a ready-made model. He or she will also produce a final product more in keeping with his or her personal taste. Therefore, rather than provide a model for people to copy, we give people the tools and materials and the basic structure or information they need to produce a product on their own. We then step back to act as resource people while they create the final product themselves. In this way teachers leave with games they have invented to suit particular needs and learning styles in their classrooms, and children leave with cars, dolls or puppets that are uniquely theirs. All people leave having learned not how to make specific products, but how to manipulate the materials independently so that they feel capable of making other things on their own as well.

This book is an outgrowth of the workshops. The ideas are taken from the most popular sessions, and the philosophy of presentation is the same. Here, too, while each idea or project is described fully with complete directions for making and using, the aim is to take people beyond the examples in the book. The book is not designed to be a cookbook whereby the reader mixes the prescribed ingredients together to make a standardized product. Such an approach would give the reader nothing that would help him or her go on to make more things on his or her own. Instead, I have tried to give the reader the basic tools with which he or she can improvise. In the Games Section I have described six basic game formats into which many different ideas, skills, and materials can be "plugged in" to make an endless number of games of the reader's own devising. Many examples, suggestions and variations are given for each. In the Crafts Section, rather than show how to make an oatmeal-box car, I have illustrated three different ways of attaching wheels, axles and car bodies together, and have offered a list of possible materials for each, so that instead of coming away with one car, the reader will have the resources for making many. In the area of Science, I have given instructions for making open-ended, exploration-aiding devices in the belief that these kinds of instruments prompt children to experiment and to learn for themselves. Throughout the book I have posed questions and raised challenges designed to take the reader beyond the given directions and to encourage him or her to explore the materials on his or her own. It is through such active participation that the best learning takes place.

All the examples in this book were originally made with industrial scrap materials from Recycle. Game boards were made from plastic trays used for molding camera lenses, from sheets of holey rubber out of which gaskets had been punched, and from rejected rolls of labels from thread spools. For markers we used cylindrical rubber shock-absorbers from bridges, parts from plastic coffee pots and reject door knobs. Dolls were made from foam rubber once intended for stereo speakers and dressed in lace and ribbon remnants from valentine candy boxes.

Most people will not have access to these specific materials. Therefore, all of the ideas in the book are perfectly workable using only ordinary household items. However, I have frequently mentioned the specific scrap item we used at Recycle in order to give people an idea of the range of uses for seemingly useless items and to give them an idea of what kinds of materials are being thrown away daily and what they might hope to find should they decide to collect industrial scrap on their own.

Any community with a small amount of local industry is a potential gold mine for materials. In addition to providing a wealth of materials for projects, collecting scrap or starting a small recycle center can provide a stimulating educational experience for both adults and children. Researching materials, making contacts, negotiating with industries, designing a suitable storage system—all offer children a chance to develop and use necessary skills by solving an exciting, real-life challenge. Locating materials can teach a tremendous amount about a city or town, prompting such questions as: Where are most of the factories situated? Are they grouped together? Why? All of which can lead to the study of natural resources, economics, sources of energy or town history.

How much material is thrown away in your town in one week? Or year? Where does it go? Do any factories recycle their own waste? These questions might lead to a study of ecology.

Do most factories make one product from start to finish? How many different places does a product go before it is ready to be used? Do any of the factories in your town use the same processes for making different things? Exploration of questions like these will open up a world of information and investigation that most people rely on daily, yet give little thought to.

Should you decide to collect materials . . .

—A trip to the town dump will show you what is being thrown away and give you an idea of where to start and what you might hope to find.

—Go to local factories, explain what you are trying to do and see if they are willing to contribute. If you know of specific items that you'd like to get, consult the Yellow Pages to see where they are produced locally and try there. Our experience is that middle-size factories are the most willing to contribute. Large industries are too busy, small ones don't have the time or staff to spare.

—Do you know anyone who works in a factory? Use any contacts you may have. Knowing the name of the Public Relations or Production Manager or President or Vice-President will mean a better chance of success.

—What is your school throwing away? Try the main office, the nurse's office and the cafeteria.

—Business offices and colleges can be sources of paper, cardboard tubes from duplicating machines, computer cards, etc.

—Hospitals throw away a wide variety of materials from their many departments: syringe cases, tubing, sterile gloves . . .

—Many stores discard merchandise: hardware stores are sources of wallpaper books and paint sample cards; stores that sell window shades throw out ends of dowels and vinyl; rug stores discard carpet scraps, cardboard tubes and bamboo poles; ice-cream parlors are a source of cardboard cylinders that make good storage containers.

—In contacting factories go in person rather than writing or phoning. This establishes your interest and makes your request less dismissable. Be dependable. If a factory agrees to give you material, show up when you say you will. Provide a box or container for them to put the scrap into if that will make it easier.

—Be prepared to accept more material than you may need and design a suitable storage system. Factories throw away large amounts of material at a time and may not want to be bothered setting aside a small quantity for you. We've often been faced with an "all or nothing" offer.

Lenny's first contacts were based on the suspicion that industrial scrap might be lucrative and plentiful enough to "recycle." Just how lucrative and plentiful it was, no one at the time imagined. Uncovering the items and discovering their variety and interest has been a tremendous educational experience for all of us as well as for our customers. I hope if this book doesn't turn you into an industrial scrounge, that it will at least engender small noises of amazement as you read about the materials, a knowing nod as you drive past a factory, and a new box next to your garbage pail for saving your orange juice cans.

Useful Tools and Materials to Know About and Where to Get Them

CARDBOARD
comes from shoeboxes, shirts that have just come back from the cleaner, the backs of pads of paper and notebooks, and boxes.

CORRUGATED CARDBOARD
is two or three layers thick with ridges in the middle. It is sturdier than plain cardboard and comes from cutting up cartons that you find behind the supermarket or the liquor store.

DOWELS
are 36" long rods available at hardware stores in many widths.

WOOD SCRAPS
are free from furniture makers and lumber yards.

CLEAR ACETATE
is clear plastic sheeting that comes from hardware stores in a variety of stiffnesses (grades).

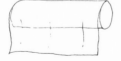

CLEAR CONTACT PAPER
is clear sticky-back plastic that you can put over game boards, etc., to protect them. It costs about 59¢ a yard at most hardware and 5¢ & 10¢ stores.

SHOEBOXES
are left behind at the store every time someone wears new shoes home. By the end of a week that builds up to quite an accumulation, which most stores are happy to share. Boxes are good for storing games and materials, for building with, for pouring plaster in for carving, and for other activities in this book.

MATTE KNIFE
is good for cutting heavy cardboard that you can't cut with a scissors.

X-ACTO KNIFE
has a finer blade and is good for delicate cutting (like rubber eraser printing stamps). Both X-acto and matte knives are very sharp and should be used very slowly and carefully.

WHITE GLUE
is good for just about everything. A trick for using it neatly is to use very little—less than you think you need. A little bit goes a long way.

RUBBER CEMENT
is good for gluing paper. The paper won't wrinkle and buckle the way it does with white glue.

GAMES

Good Materials for Making Game Boards

OLD GAME BOARDS: Paint right over them.

THE COVERS FROM WALLPAPER AND UPHOLSTERY BOOKS: Go to hardware stores and ask for their old samples. The covers of the books are extra-sturdy, vinyl-covered cardboard which you can paint over.

THE SIDES OF CARDBOARD CARTONS: This is where I get all my game boards. At RECYCLE all our "junk" comes in large cartons and I've become an institution at the paper cutter, chopping them up into neat squares and rectangles for game boards. You can try grocery stores, supermarkets, appliance stores and liquor stores, all of which are notorious for throwing out empty boxes. If they say no, check out their backyards.

MAT BOARD: Go to a picture framer and ask for his "ends."

LINOLEUM TILE: An architect walked into RECYCLE one day wielding five boxes of 10″ x 10″ multicolored linoleum tiles; he had cleaned out his sample room! They were fantastic for making indestructible boards. Befriend any architect you meet. This one also came up with ceramic tiles (good for game pieces), smaller linoleum tiles (for individual game boards), blueprint paper, paint sample cards and two slabs of industrial glass that I immediately took home to use for hot plates!

IF YOU CAN'T FIND ANY OF THESE you can make your boards out of paper and cover them on both sides with clear contact paper to make them sturdy. Then you can roll them up and store them away.

TO MAKE LARGE SIZE GAME BOARDS that you can store easily, cut the boards in half and tape the back side with colored Mystik tape. They will be attractive and fold up, but open out flat.

Good Things to Use for Game Markers

bottle caps
buttons
dried beans
pennies
paper clips
rubber or metal washers

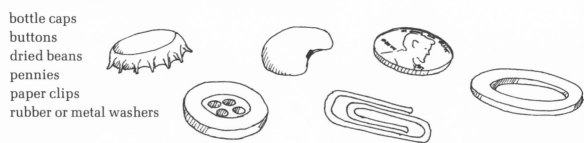

TRAIL GAMES

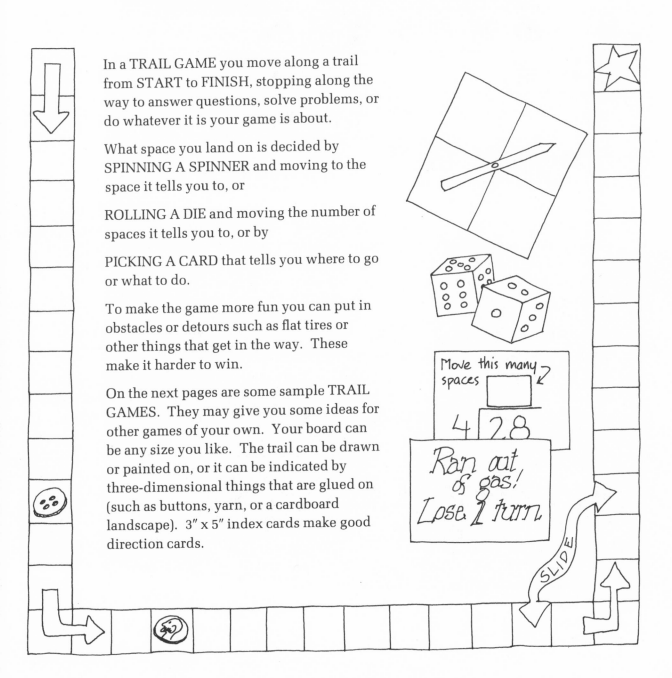

In a TRAIL GAME you move along a trail from START to FINISH, stopping along the way to answer questions, solve problems, or do whatever it is your game is about.

What space you land on is decided by SPINNING A SPINNER and moving to the space it tells you to, or

ROLLING A DIE and moving the number of spaces it tells you to, or by

PICKING A CARD that tells you where to go or what to do.

To make the game more fun you can put in obstacles or detours such as flat tires or other things that get in the way. These make it harder to win.

On the next pages are some sample TRAIL GAMES. They may give you some ideas for other games of your own. Your board can be any size you like. The trail can be drawn or painted on, or it can be indicated by three-dimensional things that are glued on (such as buttons, yarn, or a cardboard landscape). 3″ x 5″ index cards make good direction cards.

Move this many spaces

4 2.8

Ran out of gas! Lose 1 turn

SLIDE

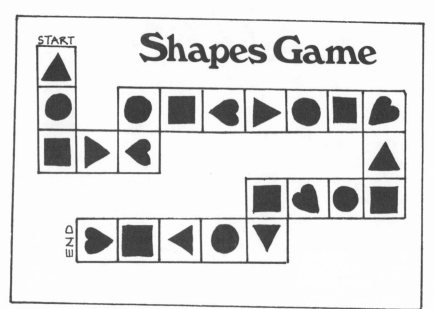

Shapes Game

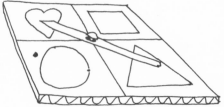

Each player has one marker to move along the trail. Spin the spinner and notice what shape it lands on. Then move your marker to the first space on the trail that has a picture of that shape on it. The next player then takes a turn. Players continue to take turns in this way until one person reaches the END and wins.

TO MAKE A SPINNER:

Use: sturdy cardboard
     a plastic drinking straw
     a paper fastener fastened loosely

Make a hole in the cardboard and the straw with a hammer and nail. The hole should be large enough so the stick turns easily.

YOU CAN MAKE OTHER GAMES THE SAME WAY:

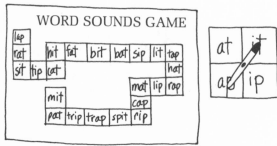

In this game you spin the spinner and move to the first word on the trail that has that sound in it.

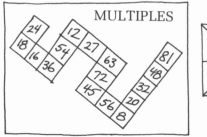

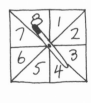

In this game you spin the spinner and move to the first space on the trail that contains a multiple of that number.

Word Trails

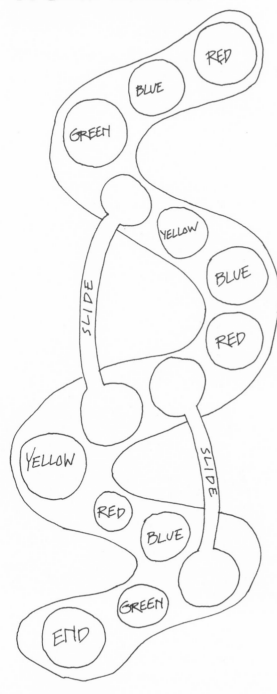

2–4 PLAYERS

THE GAME CONTAINS:

10 blue cards — blue on one side, a different rhyming question on the other side of each card, such as "What is a word that rhymes with laugh?"

10 red cards — red on one side with an antonym question on the other, such as "What's an antonym for win?"

10 green cards — green on one side, a synonym question on the other, such as "What's a synonym for late?"

10 yellow cards — yellow on one side and an "obstacle" on the other, such as "The cat chewed up your homework. Go back 2 spaces."

1 die

a playing board

a marker for each player

TO PLAY

Cards are sorted by color and placed face down. Toss the die and move the number of spaces indicated. If you land on a colored space, pick a card of that color and follow its direction. If you answer correctly stay in that space. If not, go back to the last space you were on. Then the next player takes a turn. If a player lands on a space with a slide (going either forward or backward), the slide must be taken. The first player to reach the END wins.

You can make other games like this using other kinds of questions. For example:

All red cards could ask questions about history such as: "Who regretted he had but one life to give for his country?"

All green cards could be science questions such as: "What temperature does water freeze at?"

Every time you land on a yellow space you could have to imitate an animal.

Or, you might make a game about your class in which you move along a path that represents a typical day:

Try different ways of counting dice to determine your number of moves:
- move the DIFFERENCE of the numbers showing;
- or the PRODUCT of the numbers showing (you'll need a long trail, or to go around more than once);
- or two times their sum;
- or half their sum;
- or 1/5 of their product; etc.

Or, instead of using dice, use 4 discs or bottle caps numbered 1 to 4 with 0 on the back of each. Toss them and add them up.

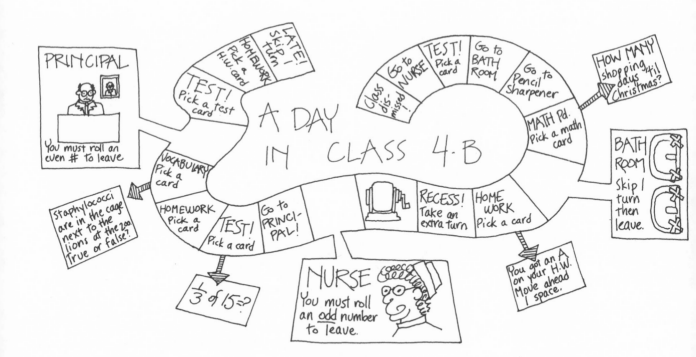

Can you make up a game about your town? Suppose you used a local map for your board? Suppose each player had $10 to spend and certain things to buy or do or certain places to go?

Divide
a
Ride

2–4 PLAYERS

GAME CONTAINS:

  a playing board
  4 markers of different colors
    (We used stripes going in different
    directions to represent colors here. You
    can paint the colors on your board and
    use buttons of the same colors for your
    markers.)
  3 dice

TO PLAY:

Choose a marker and put it on the corner
circle of your color. Toss all 3 dice and add
them up to find their total. Then pick ONE
of the dice and divide the total by that
number. Move the number of spaces of the
REMAINDER.

For example: You roll 3, 4, and 1
               $3 + 4 + 1 = 8$
               You then divide 8 by 3, by
               4, and by 1 to see which
               will give you the biggest
               remainder — so you can
               move the most spaces.

  $8 \div 3 = 2$ remainder 2
  $8 \div 4 = 2$ remainder 0
  $8 \div 1 = 8$ remainder 0
  You pick $8 \div 3 = 2$ (r.2), and move 2
spaces.

Players move counter-clockwise around the
board and up the path of their color that
leads to HOME. The first player to reach
HOME by EXACT COUNT wins.

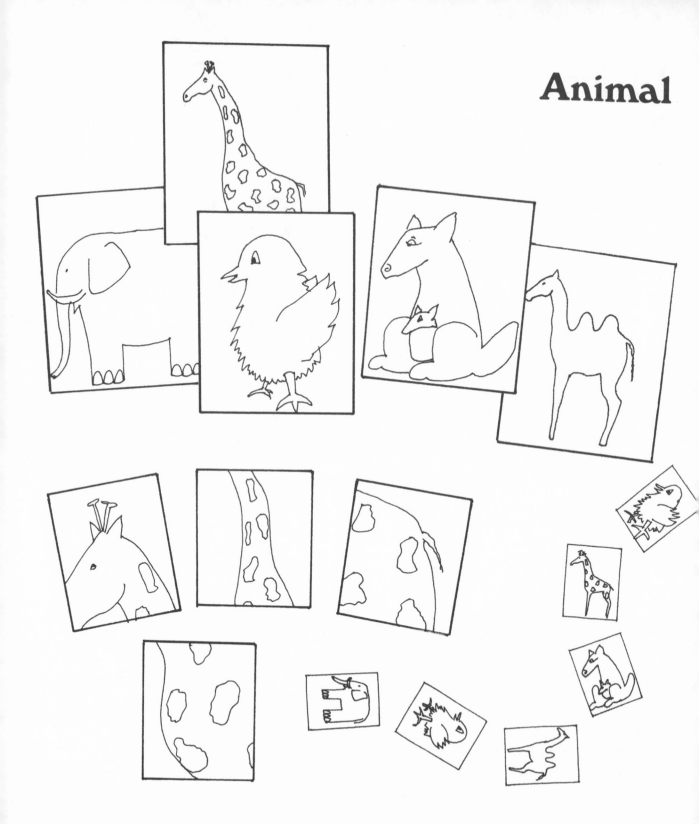

Animal

Trackers

A giant-size game played on the floor by 3 or more players

GAME PIECES YOU MUST MAKE:

1. Choose 5 animals and make 4 cards of each animal (20 cards total, each card approximately 8″ x 10″). Cover the Animal Cards with clear contact paper so Animal Trackers can stand on them.

2. Make 20 "piece cards." For each animal chosen above make 4 different parts or pieces. (Be sure the pieces look just like that part of the animal on the original card because as you play the game you must match the pieces to the correct animal.)

TO PLAY:

Choose one player to become the Animal Keeper. The remaining players become Animal Trackers. The Animal Keeper shuffles the 20 animal cards and lays them face up on the floor in a path. He then shuffles the 20 "piece cards" and holds them in his hand. Without looking at the top card he hands it to the first Tracker. That Tracker must match the "piece card" in his hand to the first card on the path that shows a picture of the animal his card matches. Once the Tracker has found the correct animal card he hands his "piece card" back to the Keeper, who places it on the bottom of the cards in his hand. The Tracker then moves to the correct card on the path.

Trackers may land on an animal that is already occupied. If a Tracker makes a mistake and walks to the wrong animal he must go back to his last place. The first Tracker to reach the end of the path wins the game.

TO MAKE THE GAME LONGER: You may add the rule that you have to move to the CLOSEST appropriate animal card whether it is in front of you or behind you on the path.

OTHER THINGS TO DO WITH THE
ANIMAL CARDS:

1. Use the whole animal cards to play
concentration. Shuffle the cards and spread
them face down on the floor. Players take
turns turning over 2 cards at a time trying to
pair up matching animals. Each time you
make a match, you remove those 2 cards.
When all cards have been matched and
removed the player with the most cards
wins.

2. How many different ways can you sort
these cards? (By animal, number of feet,
natural habitat . . .)

3. If you make your "piece cards" by
drawing a whole animal card for each
animal and then cutting each one into 4
pieces you will be able to use your "piece
cards" like a jigsaw puzzle.

OTHER GAMES YOU CAN MAKE
THE SAME WAY:

Instead of using animals and animal pieces,
use:

- Words and parts of words (prefixes,
  suffixes, roots) (blends, endings, vowel
  sounds)
- Words and their antonyms, synonyms,
  homonyms
- Math problems and their answers

BINGO-TYPE GAMES

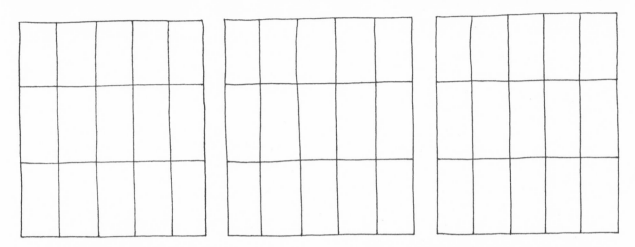

You've probably played Bingo — the game where each player has a board with different numbers on it and another player, the Caller, has a box full of numbers to call out one at a time. Each player has to check to see if the number that was called off is on his or her board, and if it is, cover it with a marker. The first player to cover his or her entire board wins.

Bingo is an easy game to make. It's also an easy game to make a lot more interesting. For instance, you don't have to match numbers. You can match pictures cut from magazines of baby animals and their mothers, 25¢ photo-machine photos of your friends and their names, flags and their countries, states and their capitals, or anything else you can think of.

You don't have to cover the whole board either. If your game is hard, you might want to cover just one line to win — or just 5 boxes that touch each other.

Your board can be any size you like. 6″ x 6″ is a convenient size. 3″ x 5″ index cards are good for the Caller's cards. So are old playing cards. If you have an old deck of cards with a couple of cards missing you can paint right over them with tempera paint mixed with a little dishwashing liquid, or you can write on the back of the cards with a permanent marker. Make as many boards as there are people playing. The boards can have some of the same things on them, but no two boards should be identical.

Make 20 or 25 cards. There should be at least one card to match every space on every board, minus any duplicates.

11

Number Bingo

ANY NUMBER OF PLAYERS

In this game you match math problems and their answers.

YOU NEED:

A board and 9 markers for each player
Caller's cards with numbers on them (see below)

9÷3	4	7-2
3×4	8+1	5
5×3	10	7

16	8	12
10+2	7	6×3
12-3	8×3	2

9	21-11	4⟌24
23+1	3×7	18
20	7	8

10×2	25-4	3×5
16	9	6×2
15-7	6	24

15-3	21	4	5	5×4
6	3	16-8	9×2	3+4
2⟌12	9	4×4	12	12-4
10-3	15	3×3	12×2	5+5

TO PLAY:

One person is the Caller. He or she shuffles the cards and holds them in a bag.

One by one the Caller picks a card and holds it up for the players to see. Look to see if the card matches a problem or an answer on your board. If it does cover it with one of your markers.

Cards can match in 4 ways:

they can be a direct match

they can be the answer to a problem on the board

they can be the problem to an answer on the board

or they can be a problem that has the same answer as a problem on the board

After the Caller shows a card, he or she returns it to the bag and picks a new one. The first player to cover an entire board wins.

Lucky Numbers

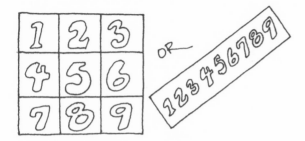

Here's a Bingo-type game that's good if you're just learning to add.

It's played a little bit differently.

YOU NEED:

    a board and 9 markers for each player
    4 bottle caps or cardboard discs
    numbered 1 to 4 with 0 on the back
    of each

TO PLAY:

Toss the 4 discs and add up the numbers that are showing. Cover that number on your board. Then the next player takes a turn. The first player to cover an entire board wins.

For a VARIATION — toss the discs, add them up, and cover either the total of all 4 discs or the total MINUS any one disc. This lets you choose your number so you have a better chance of winning at the end.

Set Bingo

In this game you match sets of shapes instead of answers and problems.

The sets have to match exactly:

VARIATION — play that you have to match backward sets — or upside down ones.

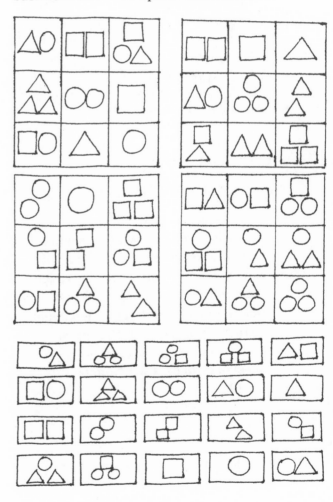

Operations

2–4 PLAYERS

THIS GAME CONTAINS:

   4 game boards, numbered 1 to 25
   (We use plastic trays with 25 small
   "cups" in them used for molding
   camera lenses. You can staple 3 egg
   cartons together cutting 2 cups off each
   one, and cutting one egg carton in half
   so that you're left with 25 cups, or
   staple 25 paper cups together, or use a
   sheet of cardboard with numbers drawn
   on it.)

   25 beans or other small markers for each
   player

   9 bottle caps or small discs numbered 1
   to 9

TO PLAY:

Put the 9 numbered discs or bottle caps into
a bag so that you can shake them up without
seeing them. Without looking pick 3 discs
out of the bag. You may perform any
mathematical operations you like with
these numbers that will allow you to cover
one of the numbers on your board.

For example: If you draw 1, 3, and 7, you
can do any of the following:

   $1 + 3 + 7 = 11$ (cover 11)
   $1 \times 3 \times 7 = 21$ (cover 21)
   $7 - 3 - 1 = 3$ (cover 3)
   $7 - 3 + 1 = 5$ (cover 5)
   etc.

Announce your equation and cover the
answer on your board. Then put the discs
back in the bag and the next player takes a
turn. The first player to cover an entire
row — either horizontally, vertically, or
diagonally — wins.

Sensiblends

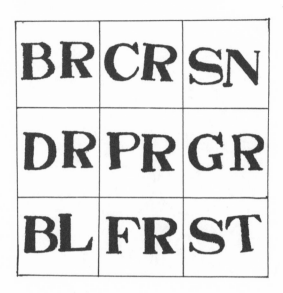

BR	CR	SN
DR	PR	GR
BL	FR	ST

A blend is a 2 consonant sound at the beginning of a word. ST is a blend; SH is not. Here are some other blends that you can use for making your game boards.

SP	FL	GR
SN	CL	GL
PL	CR	DR
PR	BR	FR
BL	Can you think of others?	

2–4 PLAYERS

THIS GAME CONTAINS:

4 game boards, about 6″ x 6″, with 9 "blends" on each. The same blend may appear on more than one board, but no two boards should be identical.

25 cards with sentences on them in which one word is missing. The missing word should begin with a blend that is on at least one of the boards. Some of the sentences should have one right answer — like, "The last day of the school week is ___." But in other sentences you should be able to fill in your own answer ("After the rain the sky was ___").

36 pennies or other small markers.

TO PLAY:

Each player has a board and 9 markers. Shuffle the cards and place them face down in a pile on the table. Draw the top card and read the sentence aloud. Try to fill in the blank with a word that makes sense in the sentence and begins with one of the blends on your board. If you can, you may put one of your markers on that space. If you cannot, your turn is over and the next player takes a turn.

CHALLENGE: If other players think that a player has given a word that doesn't make sense in the sentence (or that begins with the wrong blend) they may challenge. They must give their reason for thinking the word is wrong. The challenged player must either defend the word or think of a new one. If the players cannot agree, or the challenged player cannot think of a new word, that player's turn is over, and the next player takes a turn. The first player to cover an entire board wins.

Bingo on the Floor

TO MAKE THIS GAME:

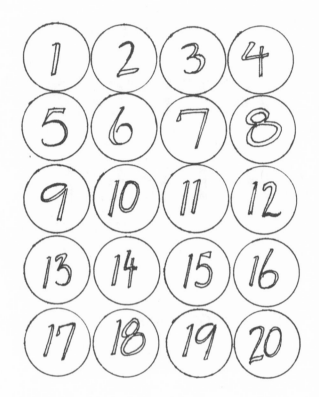

1. Cut out 20 circles of sturdy cardboard or oilcloth about 8″ in diameter, (at RECYCLE we get circular masonite punch-outs from stereo speakers which are good for this), or draw twenty 8″ circles on an old sheet or shower curtain. Make them about 2″ apart.
2. Number the circles 1 to 20, and place them on the floor.
3. Get 20 bottle caps, buttons or index cards, and number them 1 to 20.

TO PLAY:

The player who is the Caller picks a number from the bag (or players may pick their own number if they prefer) and calls it out. Player #1 has to stand on that number and at the same time touch any two other numbers which in some combination equal the number called.

For example: A player calls 18. He or she stands on circle 18 and touches 12 and 6 (or 2 and 20, or 3 and 6, etc.).

It's then the next player's turn. If a player falls or makes a mistake he or she is disqualified. The last player remaining wins.

Other Bingo on the Floor Games

PARTS/WHOLE

Make 5 sets of circles like this with a picture on one circle and different parts of that picture on 2 other circles. On 5 index cards write the names of the 5 pictures. Lay all the circles out on the floor randomly and put the cards in a bag. Players pick a card out of the bag and stand on and touch the complete picture and its parts.

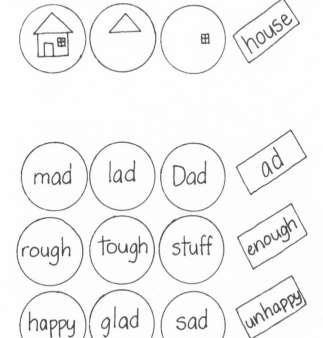

WORDS

Do the same thing with word sounds, antonyms and synonyms or rhymes.

SETS

Cut out pictures from a magazine (National Geographic has some of the best) and glue them to 15 cardboard circles (each approximately 8″) to form 5 sets of 3 members each. (For example: 3 pictures of flowers, 3 modes of transportation, 3 New York Yankees, 3 rock & roll stars, and 3 animals.) Lay the circles out on the floor randomly. Call off the name of a set and have the players stand on one and touch the other 2 members of that set.

SCRABBLE-TYPE GAMES

... in which players take turns drawing pieces out of a bag and putting them down on a board in relation to each other to make a whole.

YOU CAN PUT —

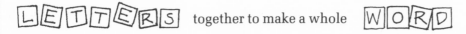 together to make a whole

Sentences together to make a whole crazy story

Pieces together to make a whole picture ...

Here are some examples ...

Six-in-a-Sentence

2–4 PLAYERS

TO MAKE THIS GAME:

1. Cut up index cards into 1″ x 1″ squares.
2. Make up 20 simple sentences such as "I am going to the store to buy some bread."
3. Print each word of each sentence on a separate card.
4. Put all the words in a box.

TO PLAY:

Each player draws 6 words from the box. Players try to form a sentence using all 6 words. For each turn a player draws one word from the box and puts one word back. The first player to form a sentence scores 1 point.

When a player forms a sentence ALL words are returned to the box and each player draws 6 new ones.

The first player to score 5 points wins.

Box of Words

ANY NUMBER OF PLAYERS

TO MAKE THIS GAME:

1. Cut 40 or 50 words and phrases out of newspapers and magazines and mount them on index cards.
2. Put them all face down in a box.

TO PLAY:

GAME I

Each player draws 6 cards.
One player begins by putting down a word to start a sentence. Taking turns, each player adds a word until the sentence is complete. (The sentence is complete when no player can add any more words and still have the sentence make sense.) If a player doesn't have a word that fits the meaning of the sentence, he or she may pass, or may discard a word and draw a new one. If the new word that is drawn still does not fit, the player may pass. The first player to use all his or her words wins.

CHALLENGE: A player who thinks that a newly added word does not fit may challenge the person who added it. That person must defend the word by explaining the meaning of the sentence. If players agree that the word makes sense, it stays. If they think it doesn't, the word must be taken back and the next player takes a turn.

GAME II
This game is played the same way as Game I except that each time a player completes a sentence he or she scores 1 point. Sentences must be at least 4 words long. The first player to score 10 points wins.

Math Scrabble

2–4 PLAYERS

THIS GAME CONTAINS:

  a playing board (see page 23)
  100 tiles numbered 1 to 10, 10 of each
    number, kept in a box or bag. (Go to
    places that sell or make bathroom tiles
    to get ceramic tile seconds.)

TO PLAY:

Without looking, draw 7 tiles from the box. Arrange your tiles to form an equation, using as many tiles as you can. You may use addition and subtraction only, but both operations may be used in the same equation. Place the equation on the board covering the ★.

No +, −, or = signs are used, but equations are recorded as if the signs were there:

means 7 − 2 = 5.

As soon as you have put down your equation, draw new tiles so that you always have 7 tiles in your hand.

When you have finished, the next player goes. He or she must make an equation which hooks onto yours.

SCORING: Each tile is worth 2 points, regardless of face value. In addition, players try to cover bonus squares on the board to earn more points:

DOUBLE NUMBER means you earn twice the value of the tile (2), or 4 points.

TRIPLE NUMBER = 6 points.

DOUBLE EQUATION = twice the value of the entire equation.

$$\boxed{7\ \ 2\ \ 5} = 6 \text{ points} \times 2 = 12 \text{ points}$$

TRIPLE EQUATION earns 3 times the value of the entire equation.

It is to your advantage, therefore, to make equations as long as possible. If you use all 7 tiles in one equation you earn a bonus of 50 points.

WINNING:

1. The first player to reach 100 points wins;

    or

2. When all the tiles are used up, the player with the highest score wins.

1	2	3	4	5	6	7	8	9	10	11	12	13	14	15
TRIPLE EQUATION			DOUBLE NUMBER				TRIPLE EQUATION				DOUBLE NUMBER			TRIPLE EQUATION
	DOUBLE EQUATION				TRIPLE NUMBER				TRIPLE NUMBER				DOUBLE EQUATION	
		DOUBLE EQUATION				DOUBLE NUMBER		DOUBLE NUMBER				DOUBLE EQUATION		
DOUBLE NUMBER			DOUBLE EQUATION				DOUBLE NUMBER				DOUBLE EQUATION			DOUBLE NUMBER
				DOUBLE EQUATION						DOUBLE EQUATION				
	TRIPLE NUMBER				TRIPLE NUMBER				TRIPLE NUMBER				TRIPLE NUMBER	
		DOUBLE NUMBER				DOUBLE NUMBER		DOUBLE NUMBER				DOUBLE NUMBER		
TRIPLE EQUATION			DOUBLE NUMBER				★				DOUBLE NUMBER			TRIPLE EQUATION
		DOUBLE NUMBER				DOUBLE NUMBER		DOUBLE NUMBER				DOUBLE NUMBER		
	TRIPLE NUMBER				TRIPLE NUMBER				TRIPLE NUMBER				TRIPLE NUMBER	
				DOUBLE EQUATION						DOUBLE EQUATION				
DOUBLE NUMBER			DOUBLE EQUATION				DOUBLE NUMBER				DOUBLE EQUATION			DOUBLE NUMBER
		DOUBLE EQUATION				DOUBLE NUMBER		DOUBLE NUMBER				DOUBLE EQUATION		
	DOUBLE EQUATION				TRIPLE NUMBER				TRIPLE NUMBER				DOUBLE EQUATION	
TRIPLE EQUATION			DOUBLE NUMBER				TRIPLE EQUATION				DOUBLE NUMBER			TRIPLE EQUATION

Word Rounds

TO PLAY:

Players take turns drawing 1 letter per turn from the box (without looking) and placing it on their playing board.

You may reject any letter you have drawn by replacing it in the box. Your turn is then over.

In any turn you may remove a letter from your board by replacing it in the box, or you may move a letter from one space to another on your board. Either of these moves counts as one turn. You do not draw another letter that turn. Your turn is over once you have replaced or removed the letter.

Words can go in any direction on the playing board:

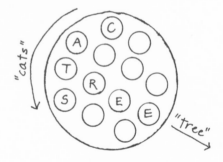

Words that can be read forward and backward (saw ⟷ was) count as 2 words. Words that read the same forward and backward (noon) count as 1 word.

WINNING:

The first player to make 4 words wins. Before winning, a player must put all extra letters not being used in words back in the box, 1 per turn.

2–4 PLAYERS

THIS GAME CONTAINS:

a round playing board for each player
62 letters (see Letter Distribution, page 25)
     kept in a bag or box

OBJECT OF GAME:

To make 4 words of 3 letters or more on the playing board. They may connect, but don't have to.

LETTER DISTRIBUTION

USE THIS DISTRIBUTION OF LETTERS FOR MAKING ANY WORD-BUILDING GAME.

A	5	G	2	N	4	U	2
B	2	H	2	O	5	V	1
C	2	I	5	P	2	W	2
D	2	J	1	Q	1	X	1
E	6	K	1	R	3	Y	1
F	2	L	2	S	2	Z	1
		M	3	T	2		

Put letters on cubes to make a "spill and spell" game. Each player "spills" 5 cubes. Whoever makes more words in 3 minutes wins.

Put letters on large cards, one letter to a card, and play anagrams on the floor.

Put them on index cards to make Word Rummy (see page 29).

CARD GAMES

Ever play GO FISH or GIN RUMMY? Then you know how to make endless different card games about words, numbers, animals, presidents . . . or whatever you like, just by substituting other cards for the ones in a regular deck.

A regular deck has 52 cards: 13 different cards (ace, 2, 3, 4, . . . Jack, Queen, King) and 4 of each card. Decks for GO FISH- and RUMMY-type games also have 52 cards with 13 different types or sets of cards and 4 cards of each type. You might have:

13 SETS OF FAMOUS PEOPLE

    4 U. S. presidents
    4 authors
    4 sports figures
    4 composers
    4 scientists
    4 inventors
    4 current events figures
      (not already in any other category)
    4 philosophers
    4 artists
    4 foreign heads of state
    4 actors
    4 military figures
    4 figures from the American Revolution

13 SETS OF EVENTS

4 things that happened this year
4 things that happened last year
4 things that happened during your lifetime
                           in this century before you were born
                           in the 19th century
4 things that happened during the American Revolution
4 things that happened during the Renaissance
4 things that happen once every day
                           once every year
4 things that are happening all the time
4 things that might happen in the next 10 years
4 things that might happen in the next 100 years
4 things that never happened

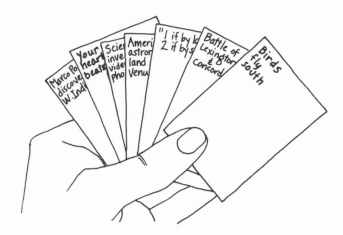

or 13 sets of rhyming words (black, tack, pack, back; hit, sit, pit, bit)
or 13 sets of matching pictures or colors or numbers or words . . .

To play GO FISH-type games, try to collect all the matching cards together into "books" by asking your opponent for a card tht matches one in your hand. At the end of the game, whoever has more books wins. WILD FRACTION DRAW is an example of this kind of game.

In RUMMY games you also make books of matching or related cards, but instead of asking your opponent for cards you pick them from a pile on the table. By keeping the ones that match cards in your hand and discarding the ones that don't, you make books and score points. RHYME RUMMY is a game like this.

Wild Fraction Draw

2 PLAYERS

THE DECK CONTAINS:

13 sets of 4 equivalent fractions and decimals or pictures:

1/2	2/4	4/8	.5
1/3	2/6	3/9	.33
1/8	2/16	4/32	
1/4	2/8	9/36	.25
3/4	6/8	12/16	.75
3/8	6/16	9/24	
5/6	10/12	20/24	
etc.			

TO PLAY:

Shuffle the cards and deal 7 to each player. Put the remaining cards face down in a pile on the table. Ask your opponent for a card that matches a card in your hand: "Do you have a card that equals 1/2?" If your opponent has such a card, he or she must hand it over. (If he has more than 1, he need hand over only 1 card.) If your opponent does not have a matching card, you may draw a card from the pile. If you draw a card you have asked for (a card that equals 1/2) you may go again. Otherwise your opponent takes a turn. As players accumulate 4 matching cards (a "book") they lay them down on the table. When all the cards have been used up, the player who has made the most books wins.

Rhyme Rummy

2 PLAYERS

THE DECK CONTAINS:

13 sets of 4 rhyming words such as:
  black, pack, back, tack
  bit, sit, hit, pit
  eight, rate, mate, wait
  stuff, tough, rough, buff
  etc.

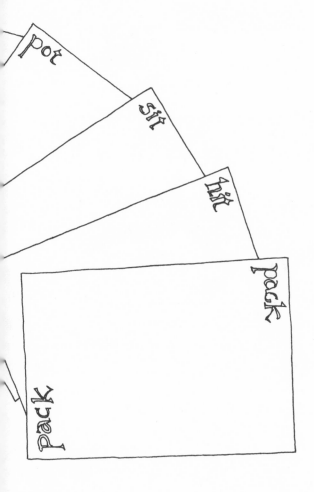

TO PLAY:

Shuffle the cards and deal 7 cards to each player. Place the remaining cards face down in a pile on the table. Turn the top card face up beside the deck. You begin by drawing the face up card, or the top card from the deck. Arrange the cards in your hand and discard the unwanted card by placing it on the face-up pile. The next player may then draw either your discard or the top card from the deck.

Each time you get a set of 3 or 4 rhyming cards you place the "book" on the table. You score 1 point for each card you have laid down in a book. If you lay down a set of 3 cards, the other player can lay down the 4th matching card and score 1 point. Play continues until all the cards are used up. The player with the highest score wins.

Use the Letter Distribution on page 25 to make a deck of 62 cards with which you can play 2 more games. Play them exactly as you would WILD FRACTION DRAW or RHYME RUMMY, but make *words* instead of matches.

Make your cards out of 3″ x 5″ index cards. Print the letters or words as close to the upper left-hand corner as you can, and then upside down in the lower right-hand corner. This will make them easier to read in your hand.

The Same Game -A Communications Game

GAME CONTAINS: 2 PLAYERS

2 sets of playing boards approximately 5″ x 7″. The boards are simplified pictures of various scenes.

Some possible boards are:

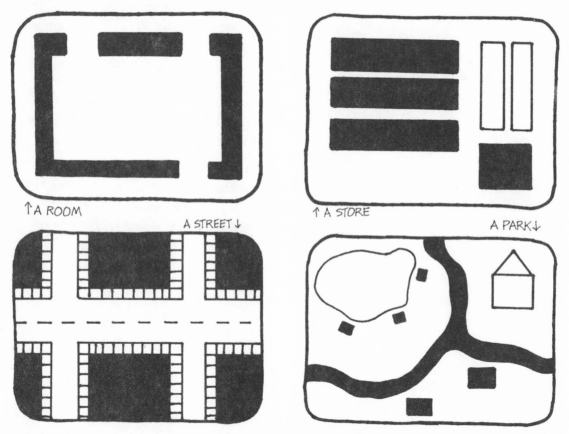

The pictures should be recognizable but not so realistic that they can only be interpreted in one way. For example, in our store board, the square in the lower right-hand corner might be a cash register or an ice-cream freezer.

A book or "wall" to block the players' views of each others' boards. (We glued 2 pieces of a picture frame together so that they formed a slot in the middle into which we stuck a removable piece of cardboard.)

A handful of buttons (or other markers) for each player.

TO PLAY:

Players sit opposite each other on either side of the "wall." They decide which board to use and each one places that board in front of him or her. One player tells a story (or they may take turns telling a story) which takes place in the locale of the board (a room, a store . . .). As you talk, you place your buttons on your board to illustrate the locations of things in your story. You must verbally communicate to the other player where you are placing your buttons, and that player must place his or her buttons on his own board in the corresponding places.

For example: a story using the Room Board — "My family just moved into a new house, and I have a room all to myself. My mother said I could put my furniture wherever I wanted, so I put my bed right next to the window on the left side of the room" (puts button in upper left corner, other player places a button on his own board in the spot he thinks the first player has described). "I put my rocking chair opposite my bed, just to the left of the door" (places button to "left of door").

When the story is finished, players take down the wall and compare their boards to see if they have put their buttons in the same spots.

VARIATIONS:

For small children: Make boards with more concrete images — body parts ("I am putting my button on the knee"), the alphabet ("I am putting it on 'C' "), numbers, colors, shapes, words, math problems . . .

Sports: Make a hockey field or a football field board and use the buttons to describe plays.

What's the weirdest story you can tell about your board? the funniest? the saddest? Write down your favorite and illustrate it.

Balance Game

2 PLAYERS

TO MAKE THIS GAME:

1. Cut an irregular shape out of sturdy cardboard and print numbers 1 to 10 on it randomly.

2. Each player should have 10 pegs or thread spools or other similar object weighing about 1 ounce.

TO PLAY:

Balance the board on a soda bottle. Take turns placing 1 peg at a time on a number on the board, scoring that number of points each turn. If you tip the board you score 0 points for that turn (or lose all your points, or half your points, or 5 points . . .) The first player to reach 50 points wins.

VARIATIONS:

Subtraction: Start with 50 points and subtract the points you cover on the board. The first player to reach 0 wins.

To make the game harder:
    use a smaller-mouthed bottle
    use heavier pegs
    print higher numbers around the outside
      edges of the board.

STRATEGY GAMES
or Math Without Numbers

In strategy games, instead of answering a question or counting dice to find out where to move, you decide your moves yourself. You plan them out — as much in advance as possible, second-guessing your opponent — to block him or her from doing what you think he thinks will help him win. This is all made harder and easier by having rules that tell you how you can or can't move (for example: markers may only move forward, never backward). So, to invent a strategy game all you have to do is pick an object for the game (what you have to do to win) and some rules for moving your markers.

Here are a few sample games and a board to play them on:

1. Get yourself 11 paper clips, 11 pennies, 2 dice and 1 friend. Line up clips on one side of the board, pennies on the other. Players take turns rolling dice and moving either one marker the total number of the two dice, or two markers each one the number on one of the dice. If you roll 2 and 5, you may move one marker 7 spaces or one marker 2 spaces and another marker 5 spaces.

Markers move horizontally and vertically only, and only forward. You capture your opponent's markers by landing on them. The object of the game is to capture all your opponent's pieces. When you reach the far side of the board reverse direction; you may still move only "forward." No jumping.

2. Just like the first game, except that instead of moving markers the numbers showing on the dice, add up the total of the dice. You may move 2 markers or more any combination of steps that add up to that total. You may NOT move only one marker.

3. Put different color dots on some of your markers, or use different kinds of markers. Give each marker a different kind of move, as in chess. Same object for game. Can you design markers that look like their moves? How might a man shaped like ● move? How about 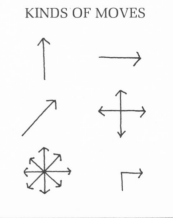 ?

4.5.&6. are for you to make up. Pick an object and create some rules for achieving it. Try some of these:

POSSIBLE OBJECTS	WHAT HAPPENS WHEN YOU GET TO THE OTHER SIDE	KINDS OF MOVES
1. Eliminate opponent's men. 2. Get to other side first. 3. Get to other side and back first.	1. You win. 2. Reverse direction and keep playing. 3. You get special privileges: can move in any direction; can jump.	↑ → ↗ ↔ ↓ ✳ ↵

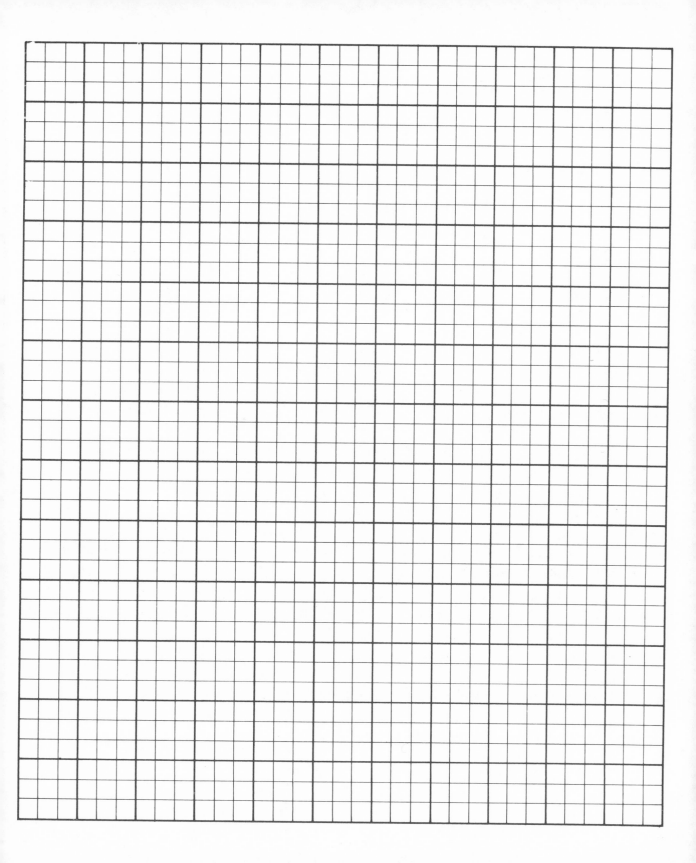

Nine-Man Morris

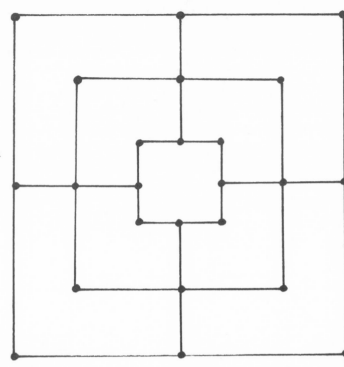

is older than the English language. One Nine-Man Morris board was found on a Viking ship, another in Ceylon (dating from the 1st century), and another in Ireland from the Bronze Age.

2 PLAYERS

THIS GAME CONTAINS:

a playing board
9 markers for each player

OBJECT OF GAME:

To remove opponent's markers from board

TO PLAY:

Players take turns placing one marker each turn on any of the dots on the board.

When all the markers are on the board, they are moved, one a turn, along the lines from one point to an adjacent point.

Whenever you make a row of 3 markers along the same line, either when entering them or moving them, you may remove any *one* of your opponent's markers from the board except those in rows of 3, which are safe.

A marker may be part of 2 rows of 3 at the same time.

A row of 3 may be formed again and again by moving a marker out and back again.

When you have only 3 markers remaining you may jump them anywhere on the board instead of moving them along the lines.

When you lose all but 2 markers, you forfeit the game.

Chinese Friends or the Sandwich Game

was played in ancient China. 2 PLAYERS play it on the same basic gameboard (see page 35), using pennies for markers. One player is heads, the other is tails. Each should have 22 pennies.

Start with 4 pennies at the center of the board like this:

Take turns putting down a penny, trying to "sandwich" your opponent's pennies between 2 of your own.

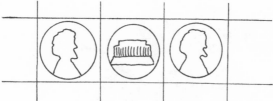

Each time you make a sandwich, turn over the penny or pennies you sandwiched so that they become yours.

You can sandwich horizontally, vertically or diagonally.

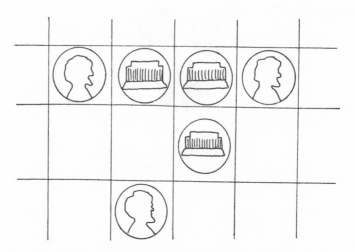

You can sandwich in 2 directions at the same time.

You can sandwich more than one penny at a time.

OBJECT OF GAME:

When the board is filled with pennies, count the number of heads and tails showing. Whoever has more wins.

Solitaire Puzzles

Solutions on page 118

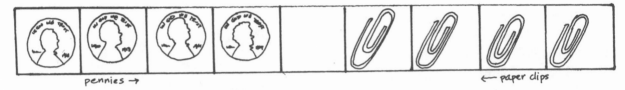

pennies →   ← paper clips

Start with 4 pennies on the left side of the board and 4 paper clips on the right side. Try to reverse the positions of the pennies and clips. RULES: pennies may move only left to right; clips only right to left. You may move into the neighboring space, or if that space is occupied you may jump over it.

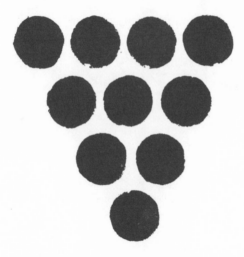

Line up 10 coins in a pyramid. Can you reverse the pyramid by moving only 3 coins?

Arrange 16 matches like this. Move 2 matches so that you form 4 squares each touching another. There should be no extra matches left over.

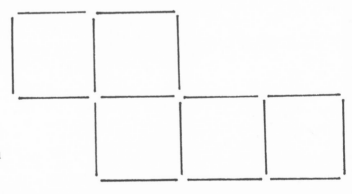

Lay out 10 coins in a straight line. Can you stack them all in piles of 2 by moving one coin at a time, and passing it over exactly 2 coins in each move? A stack of 2 coins counts as 1 coin.

Pyramid Puzzle

YOU NEED:

    a block of wood approximately 10″ long
    3 lengths of dowel approximately 5″
      long
    5 (4½″) kitchen sponges
    white glue
    scissors
    a drill

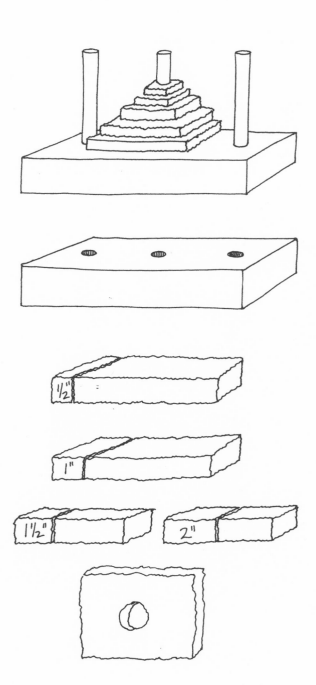

1. Drill 3 holes in the wood and glue the dowels in.
2. Cut ½″ off one of the sponges. (They're easiest to cut when they're damp.)
3. Cut 1″ off another sponge,
      1½″ off another, and
      2″ off another.
4. Cut a hole in the center of each sponge so that they will fit easily over the dowels.

BEGIN THE PUZZLE by putting all 5 sponges on the center dowel, placing the largest sponge on the bottom. The object of the puzzle is to recreate the pyramid on one of the other dowels. YOU MAY MOVE ONLY ONE SPONGE AT A TIME, AND YOU MAY NEVER PLACE A LARGER SPONGE ON TOP OF A SMALLER ONE!

COORDINATION GAMES

or

How Well Does Your Hand Know Your Eye?

The games on the next few pages test your eye-hand coordination. You sight a goal with your eye (for example, the pins in bowling) and then you use your hand, your fingers, or your whole body to help you reach the goal (by rolling the bowling ball with your arm and wrist to knock down the pins). The trick is to coordinate your hand and your eye so that your hand makes the ball go where your eye is looking.

Any game in which you aim at something uses this skill. You might:

- Put some heavyweight cartons or buckets on the floor, give each one a different point value and, standing several feet away, toss in beanbags or balls. Take a step backward after each successful throw. The first person to score 30 points wins. (For number practice, small children might toss one beanbag into Box #1, two beanbags into Box #2, and so on.)

- Cut different size openings in a shoebox. Give a point value to each hole and, standing two to three feet away, try to roll marbles into the box.

- Open a wire coat hanger into a circle and hang it over a nail in the wall. Toss in a beanbag or a foam rubber ball for indoor basketball shooting.

close up hook around nail to keep hanger on wall

Shuffleboard

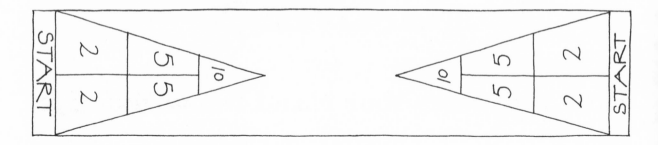

2 PLAYERS

Use chalk on the floor or sidewalk to make a board like this one approximately 7' x 2½', (or draw it on a piece of paper or vinyl that you can tape down and then roll up and put away.)

Give each player 5 jar lids (pucks). (These should be marked so players can recognize their own.) Stand at opposite ends of the board. Put your first lid in the START area on your side and, using either a stick (a tongue depressor, pencil, or spoon) or your hand, give it one long shove, aiming at #10 on your opponent's side. Shoot all 5 pucks this way. If you hit a puck you have already shot and knock it to another space, the new space counts as its final location. When you have finished, your opponent moves, shooting his or her pucks from the opposite side toward you. If he knocks any of his own or your pucks from one space to another, the new space is considered the final location (even if you have already knocked that puck). When your opponent has finished, each of you counts your score by adding up the numbers of the spaces your pucks are in. Then play another round switching turns so that your opponent shoots first this time. After 4 rounds, the player with more points wins.

Can you walk from one end of the room to the other holding a marble on a spoon? How fast you can do it? Have a relay race.

Ring & Pin

Cut the center out of the lid of an ice cream or margarine container and string it to a pencil. Swing the pencil and try to catch the ring.

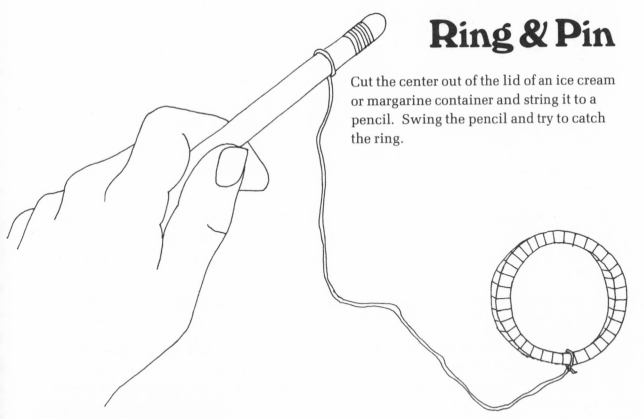

Scoop Ball

2 PLAYERS

TO MAKE:

Cut 2 shoeboxes into scoops as shown in the diagram. Glue a thin strip of wood (approximately 7" x 1") to each one as a handle. Reinforce the handle by gluing an extra piece of cardboard to the bottom of each scoop.

TO PLAY

Players stand opposite each other and use their scoops to toss a ball back and forth. No hands may touch the ball!

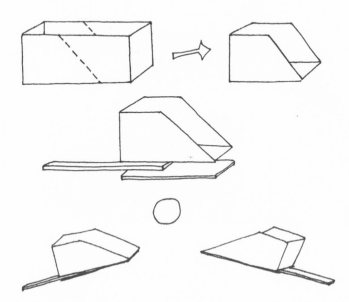

Marble Maze

OBJECT OF THE GAME: To roll the marble through the maze without letting it fall into any holes.

TO MAKE:

1. Use 2 shoeboxes. Cut 1½" from around the top of one box and turn it upside-down inside the other.

2. With a matte knife, cut a hole through the base of both boxes so that the marble can come out.

3. Design your maze: Pick a START and an END. Then draw lines that touch an edge or another line in one place only. Make as many as you like but make sure to leave enough room for the marble to roll through. (You can do this on paper, too, making a maze that you solve using a pencil.)

4. Glue strips of cardboard, rug yarn, straws, or buttons along your lines to make a path for the marble to roll through.

5. Cut holes in the maze just large enough for the marble to fall into. Choose places that will be difficult but not impossible to get around. An easy way to cut holes is to cut a star ✳ with an X-acto knife. Then pull the edges of the star up and trim them off with scissors.

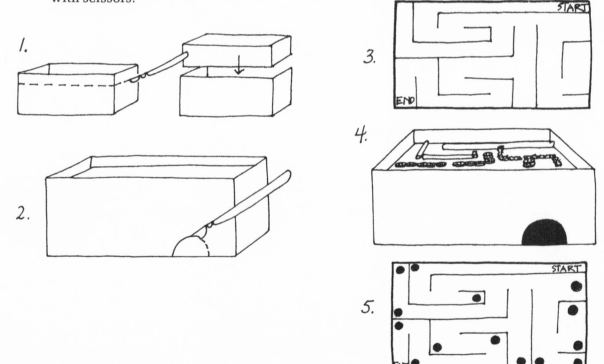

SCIENCE

MELODY INSTRUMENTS

EAR HARP

On a block of wood approximately 9″ x 14″ hammer 8 nails diagonally across the board. Attach 8 screw-eyes in a row across bottom. Fasten nylon fish line between and tighten until the strings are taut. TO PLAY: hold the instrument on your shoulder next to your ear, strings away from you, and pluck.

RUBBER-BAND BANJO

Cut a hole in the top of a shoebox and stretch 5 rubber bands across lengthwise. Pluck. To tighten the bands, hold at center between thumb and forefinger of each hand and pull out toward edges of box. To loosen pull from edges toward center.

CHIMES

Suspend different lengths of conduit pipe (available at a hardware store) from a broom or dowel balanced between 2 chairs. Or hold pipes by handles while another person strikes them. Attach string handles with masking tape to suspend them.

THUMB PIANO

Brace 8 popsicle sticks or tongue depressors between 2 blocks of hard wood. Fasten tightly with "C" clamps and pluck. If they buzz, fasten the clamps tighter.

WASHTUB BASS

Punch a hole in the bottom of a large bucket with a hammer and nail. Thread nylon fish line through the hole and tie a washer or thread spool to the inside end so it can't slip out. Attach a screw-eye near the end of a dowel or broom handle and attach the other end of the line to it. The dowel rests near the edge of the bucket. Hold the dowel in one hand and pluck the string with the other. Move the dowel back and forth, tightening and loosening the string, to change the pitch.

NAIL CHIMES

With string suspend several different size nails from a pencil. Beautiful tones!

On the Ear Harp do all the strings sound the same? Can you change the "pitch" of each string? Can you make all the strings sound the same? What's the absolutely highest sound you can get? Which string did you have to use? Can you make the shortest string sound as low as the longest one? Do you see why the strings are different lengths?

How about on the Rubber Band Banjo? What's the highest sound you can get out of it? What's the lowest? The tighter the string, the _____er the pitch, and the looser the string, the _____er the pitch.

Can you play a scale? How about "Mary Had a Little Lamb"? Five bands is all you need.

Lay lengths of pipe across 2 blocks of wood and tap them with a mallet to make a xylophone.

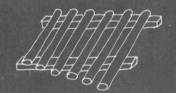

On the Thumb Piano which stick is the highest? Try to adjust the sticks to play a scale. The Conduit Pipe Chimes won't play a scale (unless you happened to get exactly the right length pipes by acccident) but they will have higher and lower pitches.

Why does moving the dowel back and forth change the pitch of the Washtub Bass? (If you want to hear some good washtub bass listen to a Jim Kweskin Jugband record.)

Rhythm Instruments

DRUMS

FOR DRUM BODIES: Construction companies use heavy cardboard tubes called sonotubes to pour concrete in. Paper companies roll paper around heavy cardboard cores. Both throw the tubes away when they're finished with them. They can be cut with a power saw to whatever height you want and make great drum bodies (also good stools, table bases, and storage units). Otherwise use an oatmeal or tinker-toy box or a carpet tube. (Carpet tubes are long skinny tubes thrown out by carpet stores. They can also be cut with a power saw.)

FOR DRUM HEADS: Go to a gas station and ask for an old inner tube from a tire. Stretch it as tight as you can (get help) across the top of the drum and tack it to the sides with carpet tacks or short nails. Or, go to a music store and ask if they have 2 old drum heads you can have. Wet them with water and lace them to the top and bottom of your drum with a strong cord. They will shrink as they dry and give a good taut "skin."

tack drum head to body or lace 2 heads together

NAIL SCRAPER

Hammer 9 nails into a block of wood so that they vary in height. With another nail scrape across them at different rhythms.

FLOWER POTS

All flower pots (even ones the same size) make a different noise when tapped with a mallet. Hang 2 (make sure they're not cracked) from a strong cord. Tie a metal washer to each of the two ends to hold the pots on the cord. Strike the pots lightly with a small mallet.

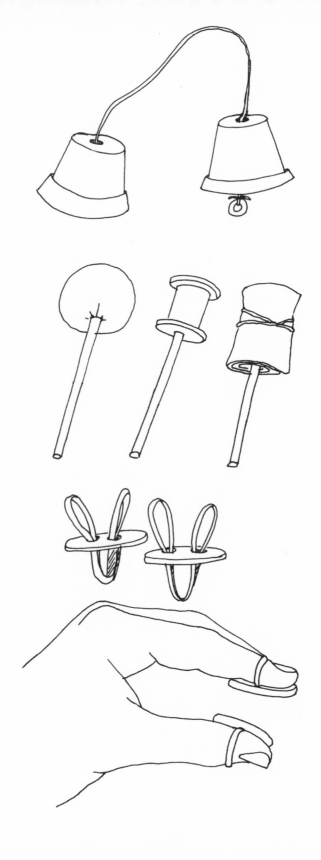

THREE WAYS TO MAKE A MALLET

I

Get a Solid rubber ball and carefully cut a slit in it 1″ deep with a matte knife. Put some glue on the end of a thin dowel or pencil and push it into the slit.

II

Glue a dowel or pencil into a wooden thread spool.

III

Wrap a piece of foam rubber, leather, or fabric around a dowel and tie it securely with a rubber band or string.

Different mallets on the same instrument will produce different sounds.

FINGER CYMBALS

Punch 2 holes in the center of 2 bottle caps (or use large buttons). Draw a rubber band through the holes. Fasten to your fingers and clack together.

RATTLES

FILL yogurt cups
       margarine containers
       medicine bottles
       small jars or boxes
       soda cans
       juice cans
       etc.

WITH uncooked rice
       dried peas or beans
       buttons
       paper clips
       a rubber eraser
       marbles
       etc.

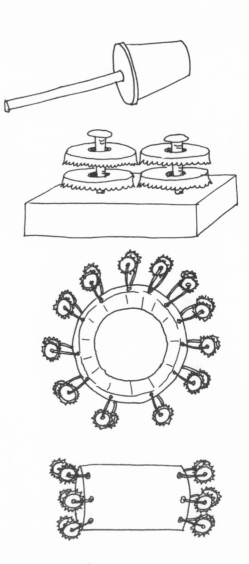

Tape the opening to seal the container, and shake. You can attach a handle by poking a hole in the top and bottom of the container, inserting a length of dowel, and taping it in place.

or

Loosely nail 4 bottle caps to a block of wood. Leave enough room for the caps to shake freely on the nail. Wobble them with your hand to enlarge the holes enough for the caps to shake.

TAMBOURINES

Glue 2 paper pie plates together, one inside the other. When they're dry punch holes around the circumference with scissors or a compass point. With a hammer and nail punch a hole in the center of 24 bottle caps. Tie 2 caps to each hole in the plates with string.

Cut both ends of a tin can with a can opener. File the inside edges so they're not sharp. With a hammer and nail, gently (so you don't dent the can) make 6 holes near each end. Also make a hole in the center of 12 bottle caps. Loosely tie a bottle cap to each hole in the can.

GETTIN' THE RHYTHM OF THINGS . . .

Count evenly 1–2–3–4–1–2–3–4 for a few minutes. Then play an instrument at the same time, one rattle, or shake, or beat for each count.

Accent the first count a little bit:
<u>1</u>–2–3–4–<u>1</u>–2–3–4

That's called 4/4 time. "Mary Had a Little Lamb" is in 4/4 time. Count and play your instrument while someone else sings the song slowly.

  Ma - ry - had- a - lit - tle -lamb . . .
  <u>1</u> – 2 – 3 – 4 – <u>1</u> – 2 – 3 – 4
(That last beat, where there was no word or note, is called a REST.)

What other songs are in 4/4 time? Try other rhythms:
  <u>1</u>–2–<u>1</u>–2–<u>1</u>–2–<u>1</u>–2 ("Twinkle, Twinkle Little Star")

  <u>1</u>–2–3–<u>1</u>–2–3 (waltzes)

Sometimes there is more than one note on a beat. Put 4 objects evenly spaced on a table. Rattle or shake or beat your instrument once over each object.

Now put another object right next to one of the four.

How would you play that? Move the fifth object around and play each new arrangement you make.

If you put down an object for each note in the first line of "Happy Birthday," where would you put them? How about "Clementine"? Try other songs.

Sometimes a note lasts for more than 1 beat:
  Down in the v - a - l - l - e - y
  1 – 2 – 3 – 1 – 2 – 3 – 1 – 2 – 3
There are really 3 beats on the first part of "valley" and 3 beats on the second part. When you sing the song you only sing one note for each part, but when you play a rhythm instrument you can rattle, or shake, or tap for each beat in the rhythm of the song.

Water Clock

Who ever heard of an inch of time or a minute of water? Here's a clock that measures them both.

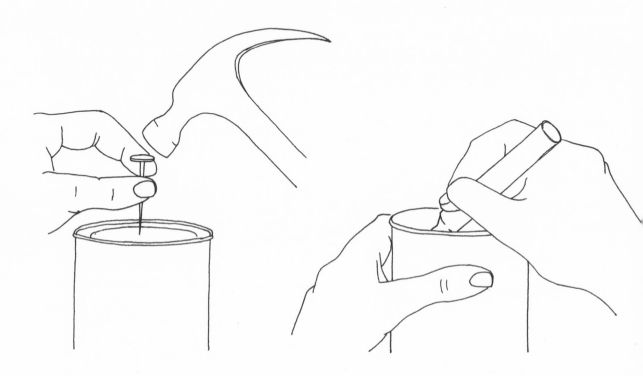

YOU NEED:

- a straight-sided jar
- a tin can (wide enough to sit on top of your jar)
- masking tape
- a measuring cup
- a ruler
- a very thin nail and a hammer
- a permanent Magic Marker

TO MAKE:

With the hammer and nail make a tiny hole in the bottom of the can. Draw a line with the Magic Marker around the inside of the can near the top. Pour water in up to the line. (Are you getting an idea of how the clock works? Play around with it awhile and see if you can figure it out.)

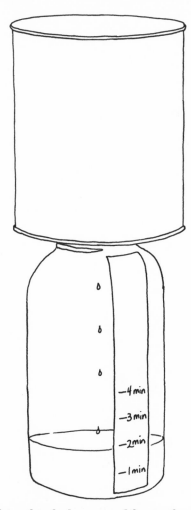

Get a friend to help you calibrate the clock. Put a strip of masking tape up the side of the jar to make your calibrations on and set the can on top of the jar.

One of you should watch a real clock while the other makes the calibrations. When the minute hand is at 12 pour water into the can up to the line. Now watch the jar. How high is the water level in the jar after 1 minute? Make a mark there. After 2 minutes? Mark and label each minute for as long as your clock goes.

Now use your clock to time things:

How many times can you write your name in 2 minutes?
How long is 1 minute? Can you tell without looking?
How many minutes does it take you to run across the yard?

How many inches of water fall in the jar in 1 minute? In 2 minutes? How many "inches of time" does your clock tell?

How many pages of a book can you read in 2 inches?
For how many inches can you stand on 1 foot?

How many ounces of water fall in the jar in 1 minute? In 1 inch? How many ounces of time will your clock tell?

Which is the shortest amount of time — a minute, an inch, or an ounce?

How many ounces does it take you to eat lunch?

Why should you always pour water up to the same point in the can? What happens if you don't?

Water Microscope

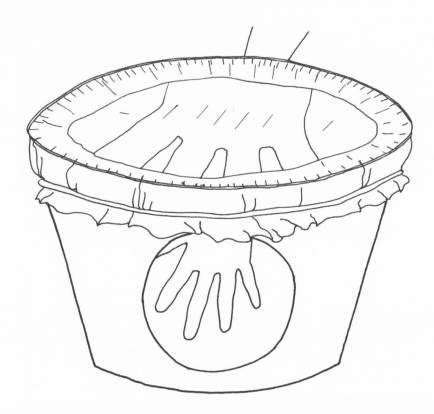

Ever look at your fingers through a glass of water? Or at the prints you left on the glass? The water acts as a lens and magnifies them. Well here's a more useful, table-top version of the same device.

TO MAKE:

Cut 2 or 3 large holes in the sides of a large plastic pail. Stretch plastic wrap loosely across the top and fasten with a thick rubber band or string. Fill the cavity with water.

Hold the object you are studying under the plastic wrap, inside the pail. What happens if you move the object closer to or farther away from the lens?
What happens if you make the plastic wrap tighter or looser?
Can you figure out how many times your lens magnifies?
What makes gray in a newspaper photo?

FOR REAL "SHARP EYES": How many steps are on the Lincoln Memorial on a penny?

Balances

TO MAKE BALANCE PANS:

USE: Milk cartons cut down to 3"; or margarine or ice cream containers; or shoeboxes cut off on one side and closed up to the size you want; or aluminum pie plates.

CUT: 3 lengths of string 15" long.

POKE: 3 holes equidistantly spaced near the top of each "pan."

LACE: the strings through and tie knots.

KNOT: the 3 strings at the top, making sure the pans hang evenly and are not tilted.

OPEN: 2 paper clips by pulling the inside loop up.

SUSPEND: the pans from the clips.

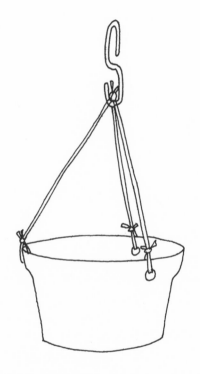

If your pans don't balance when you first make your scale, weight the lighter one with a small bit of clay, or some toothpicks or paper clips taped to the bottom.

You can use balances to help with addition and subtraction: Put 7 pennies in one side and 3 in the other. How many pennies must you add to the lighter side to make it balance? How many do you have to take away from the heavier side?

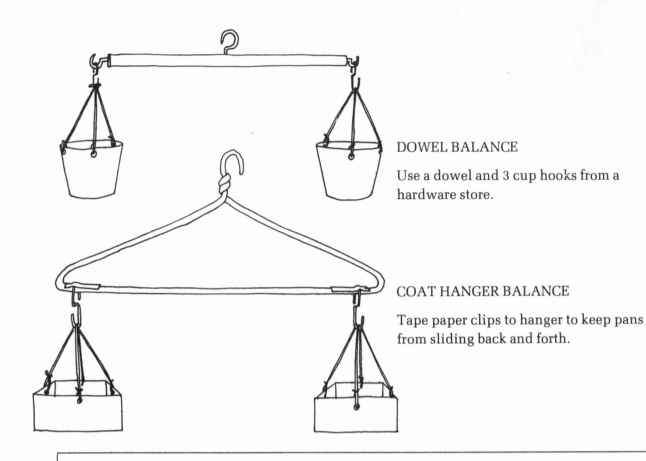

DOWEL BALANCE

Use a dowel and 3 cup hooks from a hardware store.

COAT HANGER BALANCE

Tape paper clips to hanger to keep pans from sliding back and forth.

USE YOUR BALANCE TO WEIGH OUT THE INGREDIENTS IN THIS RECIPE FOR SUGAR COOKIES.

Use medium-size household nails for weights. (Remember to subtract the weight of the container your ingredients are in.)

Cream until light and fluffy:
    48 nails of butter
Beat in:
    60 nails of sugar
Add:
    1 egg
    3 nails of vanilla
Beat thoroughly.

Add:
    7 nails of milk
Sift together and stir in:
    65 nails of flour
    1 nail of salt
    1 nail of baking powder

Mix well. Arrange by teaspoonfuls 1″ apart on a buttered cooky sheet. Bake 8 minutes at 375°. Makes 50 to 60 cookies.

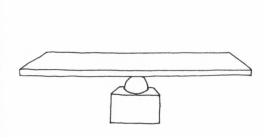
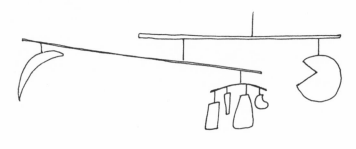

BALANCE BOARD AND FULCRUM

YOU NEED:
    a wood block about 3″ high
    a wood board approximately 3″ x 20″
      (or several sheets of cardboard glued
      together to make them rigid)
    a solid rubber ball
    a matte knife
    glue

Cut the rubber ball in half and glue half to the block of wood.

Balance the board on the ball.
Balance 2 identical objects on the board.
Balance 4 identical objects on the board.
Try 3 objects . . . 5 objects.

Now balance 2 different objects on the board.

How can you make 2 identical objects balance without having them the same distance from the center?

Can a book balance a pencil?

MOBILES

A mobile is a balance, too. Each point where a string supports a crossbar is actually a tiny fulcrum. Your experience with the balance board will help you make a mobile on a hanger.

Gather some pencils or twigs to use as crossbars and an assortment of lightweight objects (like feathers, shells, tin can lids with the edges filed, painted thread spools, shapes cut from cardboard, parts from old clocks, nuts and bolts . . .) to hang from them. Use nylon thread or button thread to suspend the objects.

Rubber Band Spring Scale

The principle of this scale is that the rubber band works as a spring, stretching more or less with the amount of weight put into the pan.

MODEL I

YOU NEED:
   a tinker toy or toilet brush box (or other
      very sturdy carton)
   a cup hook
   a rubber band

1. Cut one side out of the box.
2. Screw cup hook into top.
3. Suspend the rubber band from the hook.
4. Suspend a pan from the rubber hand.
5. Calibrate the back of the box (see below).

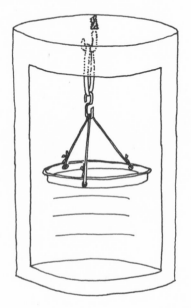

TO CALIBRATE YOUR SPRING SCALE

Put a one-pound weight (a one-pound box of sugar, for example) in the pan and mark on the box the spot where the bottom of the pan comes to. Now, gather several other objects and calibrate the scale further without using any more known weights.

HINT: Can you arrange objects in the pan so that they will weigh one pound? Suppose you put in half as many? Twice as many?

You can make a more or less sensitive scale by using thinner or thicker rubber bands. Can you make a scale that can weigh one ounce? Four pounds?

MODEL II

YOU NEED:
  a block of wood approximately 12″ x 5″ x 2″
  a ½″ dowel 1½′ to 2′ long
  a long nail and a hammer
  white glue
  a drill

1. Hammer nail ¼″ into dowel, 1″ from one
    end.
2. Drill a hole ½″ wide and 1″ deep toward
    one end of the block of wood.
3. Glue the dowel into the hole.
4. Suspend rubber band from nail, and pan
    from rubber band.
5. Tape a piece of stiff paper or cardboard
    to the dowel to make your calibrations
    on.

MODEL III

If you have shelves on brackets on your wall
you can suspend a rubber band and pan
from the bracket. Tape a piece of paper to
the wall behind the bracket so you can make
your calibrations.

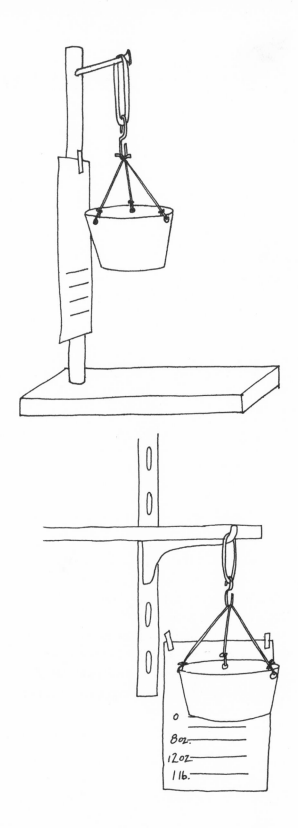

Slide Projector in a Shoebox

YOU NEED:

    a shoebox with a lid
    a camera lens
    a flashlight
    3 strips of corrugated cardboard 1½′ x 4″
    a matte knife and scissors

TO MAKE:

1. Cut a hole in the center of both ends of the shoebox. (The easiest way to do this is to cut a star ✳ with the matte knife and then to fold back the edges and snip them off with scissors.) The holes should be just large enough for the lens to fit into one and the flashlight into the other.

2. Put the lens and the flashlight into the holes.

3. Now, point the projector toward a blank wall about 5 feet away. Put the lid on; turn the lights out and the flashlight on. Move backward and forward until the image on the wall is in focus (as clear as you can get it). What are you seeing? Put your hand inside, trying to leave the lid on as much as possible. Are you starting to get an idea of how a projector works?

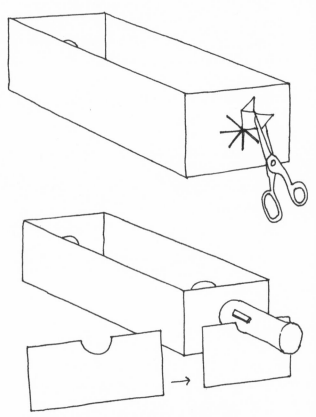

You may need a cardboard flashlight support to hold the back end up and keep the light focused through the lens.

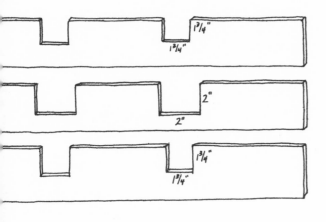

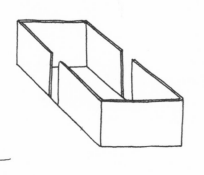

Hold a slide in the box and move it around with your hand until it projects on the wall as clearly as possible. Make a line across the bottom of the box to show where you are holding the slide. This is where you will put your Slide Carrier.

4. SLIDE CARRIER: You want to make something to hold your slides in place inside the projector. Cut openings in the 3 strips of corrugated cardboard (see diagram). Glue the strips together. Your slides (or 35-mm ones) should fit easily in the pockets.

5. To allow the slide carrier to pass easily in and out, cut slots on both sides of the box where you have made the line in the projector. (You may have to cut slots in the cover as well to make room for the slide carrier.)

6. Put the cover on the box, put a slide in the carrier and project it. (If the slide is too high trim the bottom of the carrier until the entire slide is visible on the wall.)

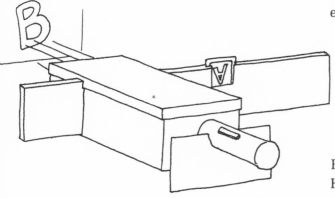

FOR FUTURE BELLS & HOWELLS:
How can you make a projector that will show picture postcards?

HINT: Remember what happened when you put your hand inside? Try some other small objects. Maybe a mirror.

61

SLIDES

35-mm slides are approximately 2" x 2". If you make your slides that size you will be able to show them in a standard commercial projector as well as in your shoebox projector.

Masking tape your "sandwich" together around the edges.

Draw on the slides with a permanent (not water-base) marker.

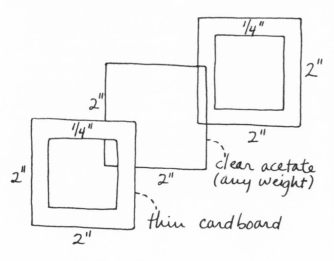

clear acetate (any weight)

thin cardboard

TRANSPARENCIES

Cut a picture from a magazine and place it face down on a piece of clear contact paper. Press the contact on firmly to get out as much air as possible. Submerge it in warm water. After a few minutes (be patient!) the magazine paper will fall away from the contact paper and the picture will have been transferred. (Don't try to rub the paper off because you'll rub the picture off as well.)

Sandwich this between cardboard frames — as above — and project.

Make slides for an overhead projector the same way.

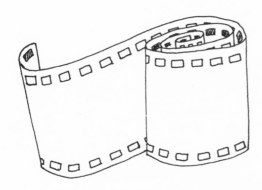

FILM STRIPS

Place on old film strip in undiluted bleach for a minute or two until you see the emulsion begin to dissolve. Pick it out with a clothespin (don't touch the bleach), and rinse it in a pan of water. Pull it through a paper towel like a ribbon to wipe off the loose emulsion. Then draw on it with a permanent marker.

Pinhole Camera

YOU NEED:

a 5″ x 7″ x 5″ cardboard box* with 2 lids
(or make a box by cutting and folding a
sheet of cardboard)

black paint or ink
electrician's tape
a pin
photographic enlarging paper (5″ x 7″)
a sheet of tissue paper
a watch with a second hand
a rubber band
glue
a bag made from heavy-weight black
fabric that light will not pass through

TO MAKE THE CAMERA:

1. Paint the inside of the box and the lid
black. (Any extra light will give a blurred
picture.)

2. Make a pinhole in the center of the side
of the box opposite the lid. This will be
your lens.

3. In one of the lids cut an opening 3″ x 5″.
Glue the tissue paper over the inside of the
opening.

4. Make a shutter by taping a rubber band
to a small piece of cardboard. Put the rubber
band around the box so that the cardboard
covers the lens and keeps light from
exposing your film.

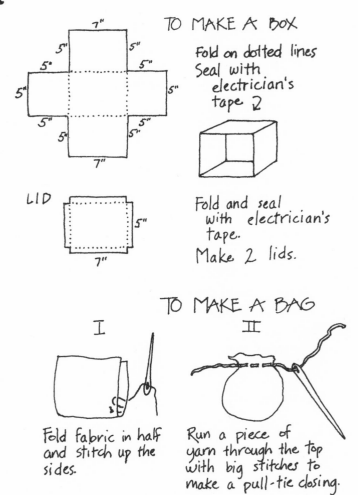

TO MAKE A BOX

Fold on dotted lines
Seal with
electrician's
tape 2

Fold and seal
with electrician's
tape.
Make 2 lids.

TO MAKE A BAG

I

Fold fabric in half
and stitch up the
sides.

II

Run a piece of
yarn through the top
with big stitches to
make a pull-tie closing.

*The camera must be the same size as the
enlarging paper. Enlarging paper comes in
these sizes:

3″ x 3½″ (hard to find, expensive)
3″ x 5″ (hard to find, expensive)
5″ x 7″ (common, least expensive)
8″ x 10″ (common, more expensive)

TO USE THE CAMERA:

1. Go into a very dark place (like a closet with the door closed all the way). Quickly, so you don't expose the paper at all, take a sheet of photographic paper and put it into the plain box lid. Put the lid into the black bag.

2. Out of the closet — put the lid with the tissue paper "screen" on the camera.

3. Go to a sunny spot to take a picture. Put the camera on a rock or wall and open the shutter. (You won't be able to hold it still enough by hand to get a clear picture because this camera takes a "long" time to expose.) Point it toward the subject to be photographed. The image should appear on the tissue paper screen.

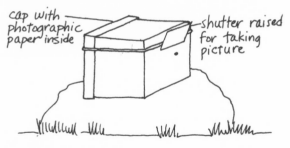

When you have the image you want to photograph notice the position of the camera (or mark it with a pencil).

4. Close the shutter and take the lid off the camera. Put the camera in the bag and put the other lid (with the paper inside) on. Put the camera back in the same spot.

5. Open the shutter and expose the paper film for 30 seconds.** Then close the shutter. Try not to jilt the camera while you do it.

6. Put the camera back in the bag. Take the lid off and the paper out. Put a new piece of paper in the lid and you're ready to take another picture.

7. Develop the paper in pans of Developer Solution and Fixer according to the directions on the packages. This will give you a paper negative. To make a positive print, put the developed negative face to face with another piece of enlarging paper. Hold them in front of a 25-watt light bulb, about 4 feet away, for 5 seconds. Then develop the second piece of paper.

HERE'S WHAT'S HAPPENING

The light rays from the scene being photographed travel through the pinhole to the back of the camera. Since light only travels in straight lines the image is backwards and upside-down.

**The amount of time you expose the paper depends on how much light there is when you are photographing and on the size of the pinhole you made. You will have to experiment to find out exactly how many seconds your camera needs in different light conditions. Try 20–30–40–50–60–90 seconds. Label each paper inside the bag when you take it out so that you know which exposure is which.

CRAFTS

CONSTRUCTIONS

Paper Logs

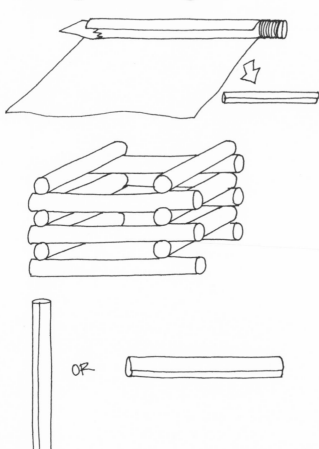

Roll a sheet of typing paper around a pencil. Glue end and remove pencil.

Glue logs together to make structures.

OR

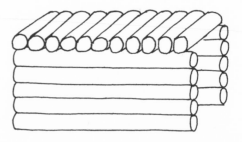

Which structure is stronger? Can you build something 6" high that is strong enough to stand on? Which way is the log stronger?

Newspaper Dowels

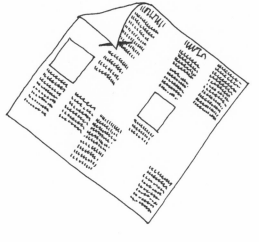

Roll a sheet of newspaper over a toothpick from one corner to the opposite one, as tightly as you can. Fasten it at the end with a piece of tape. It should be very hard and inflexible. (Some people can't roll dowels at all while other people are instantly great at it. If you have trouble team up with a good roller. He or she can roll while you build.)

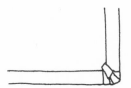

Attach dowels together with tape. Any way that will hold them is fine.

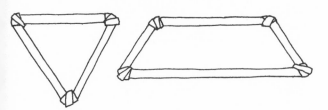

First build a frame on the floor then build up. You will have to brace it to make it stand up by itself. This is the interesting part of building with newspaper dowels.

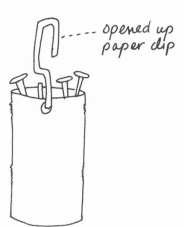

opened up paper clip

How high can you build?
Can you reach the ceiling?

Test your walls for strength by hanging a tin can of nails from them. How can you make them stronger?

Peas, Marshmallows & Toothpicks

Use dried peas soaked overnight and/or miniature marshmallows.

How high a structure can you build with 9 peas and 15 toothpicks? Do it again — is it higher this time?

What if you use 15 peas and 9 toothpicks?

Build a structure that will support a heavy book. How can you make it stronger?

What is the strongest structure you can make with 20 toothpicks and 14 marshmallows? How many books will it hold?

Build a bridge between 2 chairs a foot apart. Will it hold 5 quarters in a paper cup?

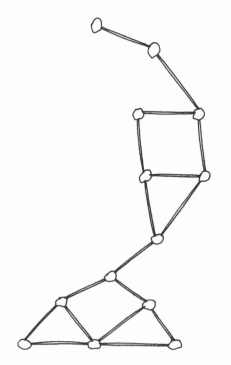

WHAT IS THE STRONGEST SHAPE?

 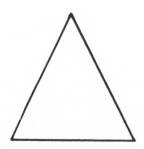 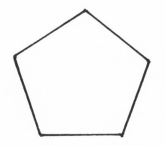 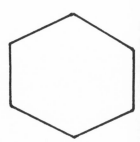

Make each one with peas and toothpicks, and wobble it. Which is strongest? How can that help you in building? Can you make a structure using only that shape?

Straws & Paper Clips

Open a paper clip  and widen slightly the narrower of the 2 ends.

Wedge each end into a plastic straw to join them.

You can bend the clip to change the angle.

Insert more than one clip into a straw to attach several straws together.

What's the tallest structure you can build with 8 straws and 12 clips?

Build a house 2′ tall.

What's the strongest part?

Test it with a cup of nails.

Build a bridge between 2 chairs 2′ apart. Will it hold a book?

Make a model for a structure in straws and have a friend duplicate it in newspaper dowels.

BOOKMAKING

These directions make a hard-cover, bound book 6″ x 9″.

YOU NEED:
  2 sheets of cardboard 6″ x 9″ (for covers)
  a strip of cardboard 9″ x ¾″ (for the spine)
  15 sheets of 8½″ x 11″ paper (for the pages)
  paper, leather or fabric to cover the cover and for the inside end pages
  heavy duty thread; a needle; colored Mystik tape; glue (or rubber cement)

MAKING THE COVER

Cut the paper to cover your book covers about 2″ larger on all sides than the sheet of cardboard and lay the cardboard in the center of it. Fold the corners over as in the diagram, keeping the edges of the folded corner horizontal and vertical. Paste them down with a dab of glue. Now fold the edges over and paste them down. You should wind up with 4 neat corners, just like the corners of real clothbound books. Do this with both covers.

Try making SHAPED books. What does the shape, or size, suggest about the content? A tiny book about tiny things, a triangular book about triangular objects . . . How about a book with holes in some of the pages that let you see what's on the next page?

Design books for younger kids.
Write autobiographies.
Make word or number books . . .

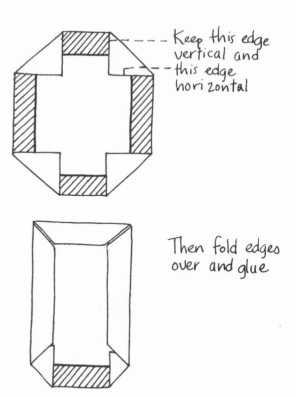

Keep this edge vertical and this edge horizontal

Then fold edges over and glue

ATTACHING THE SPINE

Cut a piece of Mystik tape 11½ inches long and lay the strip of cardboard in the center of it. Lay the 2 covers on either side of it, leaving a small space between them just large enough to allow the book to open and close easily. Fold the ends of the tape over.

THE INSIDES

Fold all the paper for the pages in half. In groups of 5 sheets sew them together up the fold using a big running stitch. Be sure to keep the knot on the outside of the fold so it won't show in the finished book. When you've sewn up all 3 groups of pages ("signatures") put a little bit of glue along the folded edges and hold them tightly together for a few minutes (2 groups at a time), until the glue sets. This will hold your signatures together. While they are drying cut 2 pieces of 8½" x 11" decorative paper for the inside end pages.

Place the signatures in the center of the cover (opened flat). Paste half of one of the end pages to the first page of the signatures and the other half to the inside front cover. Do the same at the back of the book. This is what holds the pages in the book.

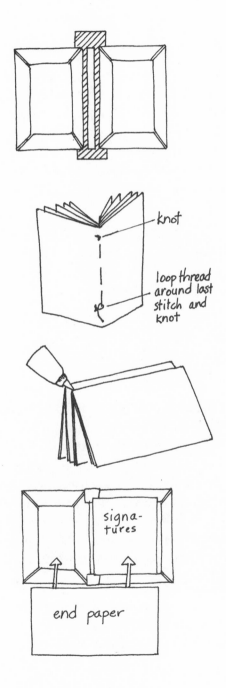

knot

loop thread around last stitch and knot

signa-tures

end paper

Here are some variations which are easier
for younger kids to make:

RUBBER-BAND-BINDING

Make a completed cover and spine as for the
first book and cover the inside with
decorative paper. Fold paper for the pages
in half. Instead of sewing them in, fasten
them to the spine with a rubber band. This
way the pages are removable and can be
replaced whenever necessary.

OR — Use heavyweight paper or oak tag for
the cover, slightly larger than the paper
you're using for pages. Fold it in half. Fold
the pages in half and fasten them to the
cover with a rubber band.

FOLD-OUT BOOK

Cover the book covers the same way. Fold
the pages in half and glue the right half of
one to the left half of the next so that you
have one long continuous sheet of paper.
Paste one end to the inside front cover and
accordion-fold the rest. Paste the other end
to the back cover. You must make an ODD
number of folds (an even number of pages)
in order for the back cover to fit on the right
way.

Use the book to illustrate a progression —
from large to small, from one color to
another, from one word to another.

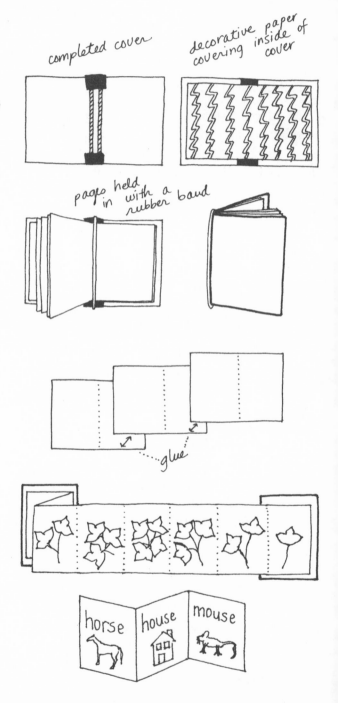

PRINTING

Stamps

MAKE A STAMP PAD by cutting a milk carton down to 3″ high and putting a sponge inside. Pour tempera paint onto the sponge. Press objects onto the sponge, then onto paper.

YOU CAN PRINT WITH ALMOST ANYTHING:

fruits and vegetables

potatoes can be carved with a butter knife to make a raised design

erasers

can be carved very slowly with an X-acto blade

fingers
feet

kitchen utensils

anything is worth a try

RUBBER makes the best stamps. Go to a gas station and ask for OLD INNER TUBES from tires. (You may have to try several gas stations — inner tubes are getting rare.) If you can't get an inner tube use cardboard instead.

----thread spool handle

Cut a shape out of the rubber tube and glue it to a block of scrap wood or a piece of cardboard. Press it into a stamp pad and then onto paper.

MAKE ALPHABET STAMPS

to print letters
       a newspaper
       a book

make the letters backwards or else they will print backwards

to make alphabet pictures

OR MAKE UP A NEW LANGUAGE AND PRINT IT

You can do this by substituting another letter or a symbol for each letter of the alphabet:

A	B	C	. . .	X	Y	Z
Z	Y	X	. . .	C	B	A

Z = A, Y = B, etc.

Or you could invent symbols for common words or ideas:

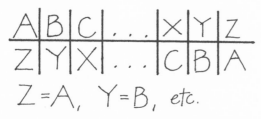

= eye or I

= sunrise or morning

DECIPHER THIS:
XLMTIGFOZGRLMH HSVIOLXP !

WHAT DOES THIS MEAN?

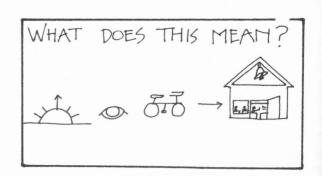

MAKE NUMBER STAMPS

to print math problems
or to print number cards for kids who are
     just learning to count

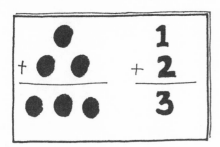

PRINT GAME BOARDS FOR GAMES YOU
  MAKE

The ancient Greeks wore rings with raised
designs on them, which doubled as printing
stamps. Try designing your own ring
symbol. See if you can make it represent
you so well that other people know it's
yours without asking. (What do people
associate with you? Do you have any
peculiar habits? Clothes? Pets?)

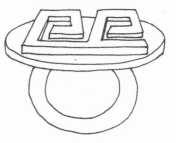

How many different patterns can you make
from one shape? The whole next page was
printed with this one stamp.

Block Printing

START: with a base of cardboard.

GLUE ON: rubber (from an inner tube)
     cardboard
     fabric
     yarn or string

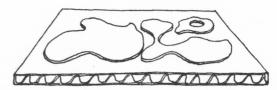

Make the surface the same height all over or
else only the highest areas will print.

USE: printing ink and a brayer to ink the
   block (see diagram); or paint the
   block with tempera paint and a
   sponge.

PRESS: the block onto paper and rub the
    back of the block firmly with your
    hand.

TO INK THE BLOCK

squeeze ink out on a cookie sheet or other flat surface

spread it with a brayer until it feels "tacky"

roll the brayer over the block

press the block on paper and rub

Rollers

USE: cardboard juice cans
   tin cans with their labels on
   paper towel tubes
   toilet paper tubes

GLUE ON: rubber (from an inner tube)
     string
     fabric
     leather

ROLL: the roller through ink or paint
   and across paper to make
   repeating patterns.

Corrugated Cardboard

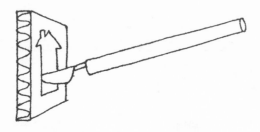

1. Draw a picture or design on a piece of corrugated cardboard.

2. With an X-acto or matte knife carefully cut along the outlines of your picture. Cut through only the top layer and the corrugations — not all the way through to the other side of the cardboard.

3. Peel off some areas of the top layer to expose the corrugated surface. These areas will print as wavy lines.

In other areas cut out the corrugations, too. These areas won't print at all.

Wherever you leave the top layer unpeeled it will print solid black (or whatever color your ink is).

4. Ink the cardboard with printing ink and a roller or with tempera paint and a sponge.

5. Press it onto paper. Rub the back with your hand. Lift off the cardboard.

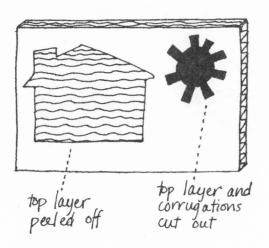

top layer peeled off

top layer and corrugations cut out

Etching

Use a Styrofoam meat tray from the supermarket for this.

1. Draw a picture on the inside of the tray with a ballpoint pen — the same way you would on paper.

2. Ink the tray with printing ink or tempera paint.

3. Press a piece of paper into the tray and rub the back with your hand.

Rubbings

Do rubbings of anything with a raised surface — coins, tree bark, gravestones, moldings, tire treads, manhole covers, leaves, etc.

Put a piece of paper over the object and rub the paper with the side of a crayon (take all the paper off), the side of a piece of charcoal, or a pencil (for small rubbings).

How many different textures can you find in the room you're sitting in right now?

Go for a walk and do rubbings of 10 things outside. You may find out some interesting things about your city or town.

MATCHING GAME

Do rubbings of 10 different leaves. Sandwich each of the leaves between a sheet of heavy paper or cardboard and clear contact paper. Put all the leaves and rubbings into a box. Have someone else match them up.

Do the same thing with textures in a room. Make rubbings of 10 things in one room. Give them to someone else and see if he or she can find the 10 things you rubbed.

grater

paper shapes

strainer

Simple Silk Screening

YOU NEED:

a sheet of thin cardboard about 8" x 10"
(a shoebox lid with the rim cut off is
fine)

very thick tempera paint (if you use
powdered paint, mix it with very little
water; if you use liquid paint thicken it
with a little cornstarch)

a piece of organdy slightly larger than
your cardboard

masking tape

a sheet of typing paper (or any paper with
a smooth finish)

a spoon

scissors

TO MAKE THE SCREEN:

1. Cut a window in the cardboard. Leave at least a 1½" frame around the outside. (How big the opening is determines how big your print will be.) Take the piece you cut out of the center and cut it in half. This will be your "squeegee."

2. Lay the cardboard in the center of the piece of organdy. Fold the top edge of the organdy over the cardboard and tape it down. Pull the lower edge of the organdy tight (but don't bend the cardboard). Fold it over and tape it down.

Do the same with the side edges. The organdy should be tightly stretched across the cardboard.

3. Put masking tape around all 4 edges of the opening in the cardboard. (Tape the cardboard to the organdy.)

Press the tape down really well. (This will prevent the paint from seeping under the cardboard and blotching your print.)

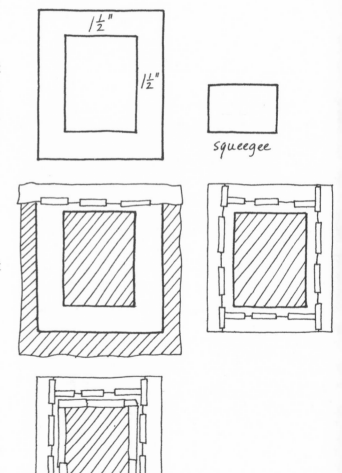

squeegee

TO PRINT:

1. Cut a shape out of typing paper a little smaller than the opening in your screen.

2. Sandwich the shape between the screen and the paper you're going to print on.

3. Spoon some paint across the top of the screen.

4. Holding it in 2 hands, use the "squeegee" to draw the paint across the screen. Press down firmly and slowly pull it toward you. Do this several times until the whole opening is covered with paint.

Where the paper shape is, the paint can't get through to your paper.

5. Lift the screen up and peel your print off. You can leave the paper shape stencil in place and make more prints or peel the stencil off and make a new one.

Make a 2 or 3 color print by using a separate screen for each color. A screen is good for about 20 prints. After that you can wash the organdy and re-use it on a new cardboard.

EXPERIMENT with positive and negative stencils.

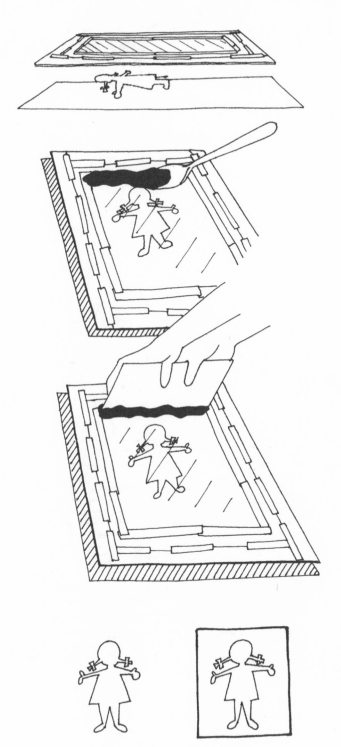

WEAVING

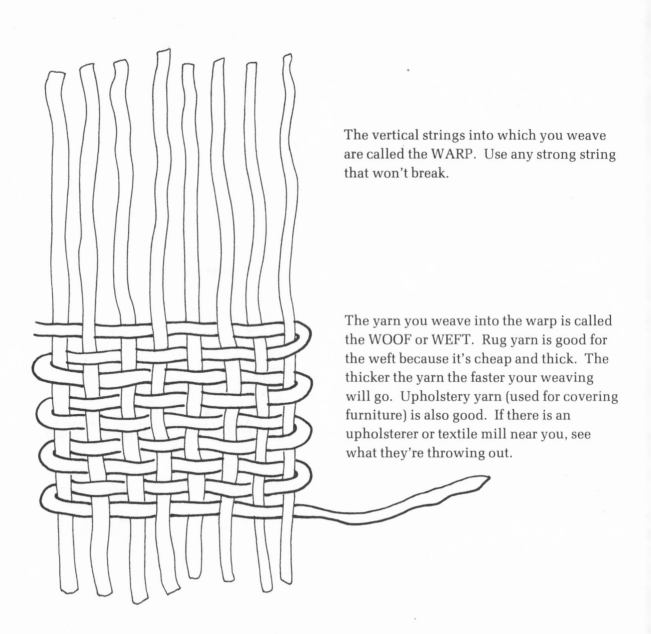

The vertical strings into which you weave are called the WARP. Use any strong string that won't break.

The yarn you weave into the warp is called the WOOF or WEFT. Rug yarn is good for the weft because it's cheap and thick. The thicker the yarn the faster your weaving will go. Upholstery yarn (used for covering furniture) is also good. If there is an upholsterer or textile mill near you, see what they're throwing out.

Paper Weaving

is a good place to start if you've never tried weaving before.

1. Fold a piece of paper in half and make cuts from the fold out to about 1″ from the edge. Open the paper. This will be your "warp."

2. From another piece of paper cut long narrow strips to weave in and out of the warp.

3. To make your weaving more interesting you can vary the width of the spaces between your warp cuts, or make your warp cuts wavy.

You can also vary the width and shape of the strips you weave in.

Use several different colors of paper.

4. To finish, glue or staple the strips in place along the edges.

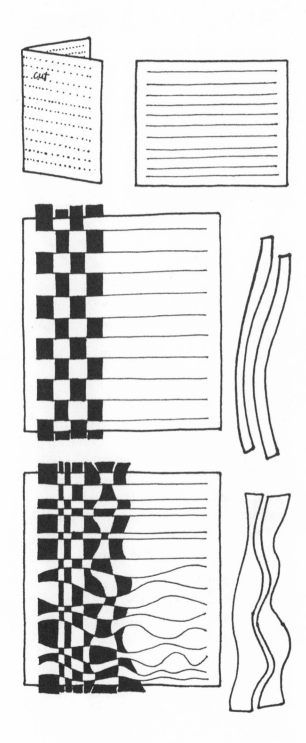

Shoebox Loom

This is a good loom for a first project because it's small and you can finish something on it quickly. It will give you a finished piece of material about 10″ x 5″.

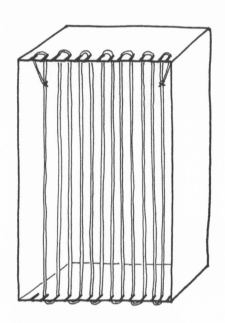

1. With scissors cut slits about ½″ deep and about ½″ apart along the two short edges of a shoebox.

2. Use a piece of strong string and wind it in and out of the notches across the front of the box. Tie each end onto the string right next to it.

3. Cut a strand of yarn about 1½′ long. Weave it under and over the warp strings alternating every other string. Pull it all the way through until the end is in the middle of the box (see diagram). When you get to the edge turn back and start a second row. Make sure you go over every string you went under in the first row and under every string you went over in the first row.

When you finish the piece of yarn start a new one the same way. You don't have to tie them together — just weave the new strand right in.

Every 3 rows or so push the new rows down gently with your fingers so you don't have gaps.

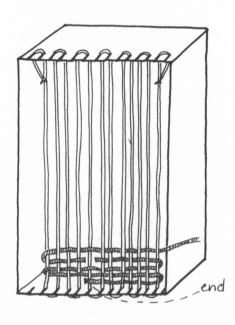

end

4. To remove the weaving from the loom, carefully slip it off the notches. If you have woven all the way to the top of the box there should be no extra warp string showing and your weaving should be tight. If it is too loose, or if you didn't weave all the way to the top of the box, carefully cut the warp strings at the top, just 2 at a time, and tie them together. This will hold the weaving in place and give you fringe.

tie the last string in with the 2 next to it

Milk Carton Loom

You can make an even smaller, quicker loom on a ½-gallon milk carton.

1. Cut out one side of the carton leaving ½" at the top and bottom.

2. Cut ½" notches, ½" apart at the top and bottom.

3. Bend the notches up so that you can wind your warp string around them.

Put on the warp the same way as on the shoebox loom.

4. Then bend the slits back and tape them to the carton to hold the string in place.

5. Weave on this loom just as on the shoebox loom. To remove weaving, untape the notches and take weaving off.

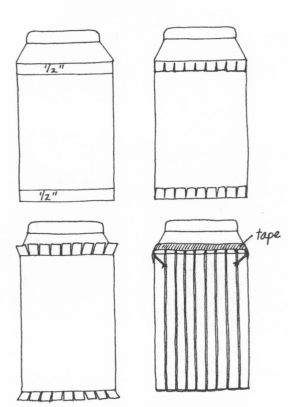

½"

½"

tape

Cardboard Loom

1. Cut ½″ notches, ½″ apart, across the top and bottom of a sheet of stiff cardboard. (Weaving is slow. The smaller your loom, the quicker you'll be done, so don't use a piece of cardboard much larger than 8″ x 10″.)

2. Wind your warp across one side of the cardboard. Tie the ends off as shown in the diagram.

3. Weave just as you did on the shoebox loom. You may find it easier to move in and out of the warp strings if you thread the yarn on a needle.

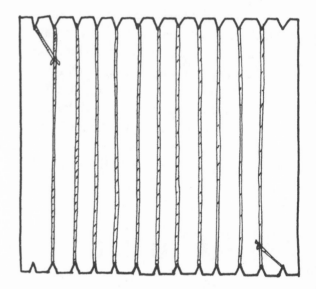

YOUR LOOM CAN BE ANY SHAPE

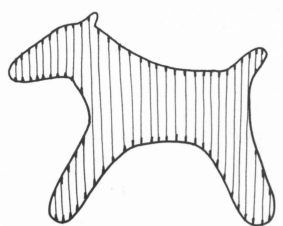

It helps to draw parallel lines on the cardboard where your warp strings will go before making your notches.

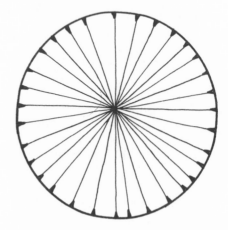

On a circular loom you must have an _odd_ number of notches.

TO MAKE A BAG:

1. Use a square or rectangular piece of cardboard. Cut an ODD number of notches ½" apart at the top and bottom. Start the notches close to the side edges of the cardboard.

2. Wind your warp around the front AND THE BACK of the cardboard. Tie off the ends the same way.

3. Weave row 1 across side A, then turn over and continue weaving on side B. Make sure that if your last thread on side A was OVER the warp string that your first one on side B is UNDER it.

When you reach the end of the row on side B, don't turn the cardboard over. Weave BACKWARD (right to left). When you get to the end of the row, turn over and continue weaving on side A. Make sure again to go over the warp string if your last thread on side B was under it, or under the warp string if your last thread on side B was over it.

When you get to the left edge of side A don't turn the cardboard over. Weave back, left to right, just as you did the first time.

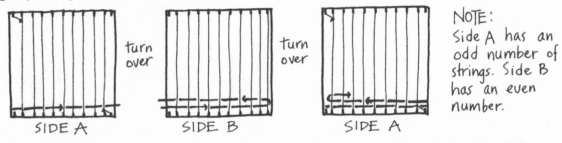

turn over

turn over

SIDE A   SIDE B   SIDE A

NOTE:
Side A has an odd number of strings. Side B has an even number.

Keep weaving this way until you get to the top of the cardboard. One whole edge of the cardboard will be exposed.

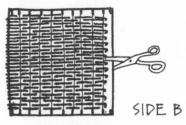

SIDE B

4. To remove the bag from the loom, cut the cardboard down the center. Gently work the strings out of the notches with your fingers and pull the cardboard out. Your bag will be already made!

5. Make a handle by braiding some yarn and sewing it on (or weave a strap on the straw loom; see page 89).

Frame Loom

Nail 4 wooden slats together or use a picture frame or a canvas stretcher.

Hammer small nails ½" apart across the top and bottom.

Wind your warp around the nails, tying it onto the first nail and the last nail with a knot.

Weave on it the same way as on the shoebox loom.

To remove the weaving from the loom:
- slip the warp strings over the nails if you can, or
- cut the warp strings at the top and bottom, 2 at a time, and tie every 2 together, or (if all else fails)
- pull out the nails.

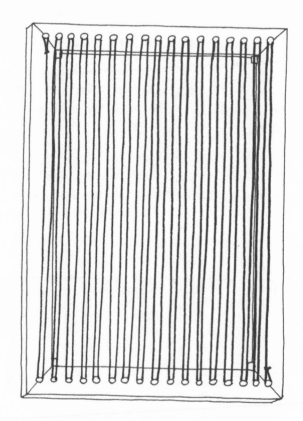

TO HELP YOU WEAVE make yourself a cardboard SHUTTLE. Wind your yarn on it so that you can use a longer length of yarn at one time.

Strings & Straws

This is a good way to make a belt or guitar strap.

YOU NEED:
  2 or 3 plastic drinking straws cut in half;
  thick yarn

1. Cut as many lengths of yarn as you have straw halves (4 or 6). Each length should be 10" longer than you want your belt to be.

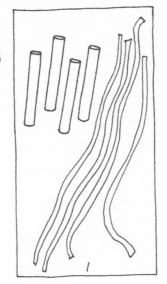

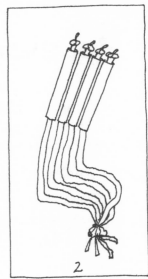

2. Insert a length of yarn and "sip" it through the straw until it comes out the other end. Make a fat knot at the end to prevent the yarn from falling back through the straw. Tie all the strings together in one loose knot at the bottom.

3. Hold the straws flat in your hand. (It may help to tape them loosely with a piece of masking tape until you've woven a bit.) Cut a piece of yarn 2' long and tie it onto one of the inside straws. Now weave back and forth in and out of the straws, moving up the straws. Try not to weave too tightly!

To start a new piece of yarn, tie it onto the end of the first piece.

When the straws are covered push the weaving down onto the strings.

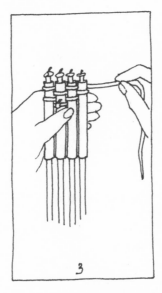

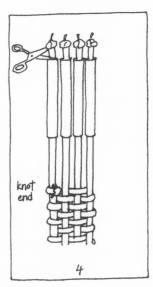

4. When your belt is as long as you want it, push all the weaving onto the strings. Cut the strings just below the knots and remove the straws. Tie every 2 strings together in a double knot. Open the knot at the bottom of the belt and do the same thing there.

5. Cut all the fringe to an even length . . . and wear it!

Popsicle Stick Loom

On the cardboard, box, and frame looms you have to separate the warp threads by hand. That's fine for a small project like a wall hanging or a bag but for a big project like a blanket or a rug it would be pretty impractical. So floor or table looms have HEDDLES that do it for you.

The heddles separate the warp into SHEDS so you can pass your yarn through in one swoop.

With Popsicle sticks you can make a loom that is really a heddle bar. It's good for making long narrow pieces of material like belts. This kind of loom is used by South American Indians and is called a BACKSTRAP LOOM. You'll see why.

YOU NEED:
    10 Popsicle sticks
    a drill with a ⅜" bit (approximately)
    white glue

TO MAKE THE LOOM:

1. Drill a hole in the center of 8 of the Popsicle sticks.

2. Glue the 10 sticks together.

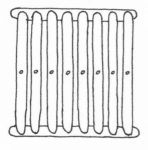

TO THREAD (OR WARP) THE LOOM

1. Cut 15 pieces of yarn twice as long as you want your belt.

2. Thread 8 of the pieces through the holes in the sticks, and 7 through the spaces between them.

3. Tie all the strings together in a loose knot at each end.

4. Take a different color piece of yarn about 1½' long and tie it loosely around the yarn at one end, just inside the knot. Do the same thing at the other end with a piece of yarn 3' long.

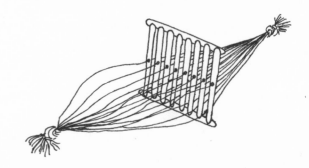

TO WEAVE:

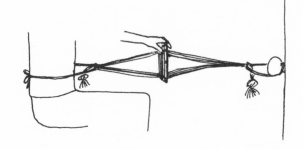

1. Tie the shorter (1½') yarn to a doorknob and the longer (3') yarn around your waist. Sit far enough away from the door so that the strings are taut.

2. Lift up the Popsicle stick heddle bar. Do you see how it separates the strings? Put your free hand into the space and pull it toward you to "clear the shed." Now pass a piece of yarn (about 2' long) through the shed from right to left. Leave about 1" sticking out on the right side.

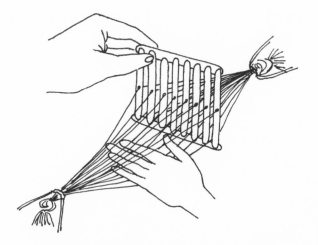

3. Now lower the heddle bar. The strings will separate the other way. (Do you understand why?) Clear the shed with your hand, then pass the yarn through from left to right.

4. Raise the bar to change the shed again. Clear it with your hand and pass the yarn through from right to left. Try not to pull the yarn too tight each time.

5. Keep weaving like this until your belt is as long as you want it.

To start a new piece of yarn just tie it onto the end of the old one.

When you have woven so far toward the door that it's hard to reach comfortably, untie the string around your waist. Take it off the strip of weaving and tie it back on near the part you're working on. Then tie it back around your waist.

6. To take the weaving off the loom, untie the loose knots at the ends of the warp strings and remove the heddle bar. Knot every 2 warp strings together. Trim fringe to an even length.

It usually takes at least 3 or 4 inches of lumpy weaving before your belt begins to look even and smooth. You might want to do a practice run first.

CAUTION: This loom has been known to create such side effects in its users as cramped fingers, a stiff back and severe irritability. Be patient!

WEAVING IMPROVES HANDWRITING!

When you weave you use your hands and fingers in very much the same way that you do when you write. So for kids who are just learning to write or who get their letters returned because the mailman can't read the address, weaving is good practice!

Weaving tools were found in the pyramids of ancient Egypt. They are 4,000 years old.

Where does yarn come from?

YOU'RE IN GOOD COMPANY WHEN YOU WEAVE!

For thousands of years people have been weaving on frame looms and backstrap looms like the ones here. Until recently (that is, the sixteenth century when knitting became popular), weaving was the main way people made cloth to keep themselves warm, to warm their houses and to hold their possessions. But people often used their weaving to tell stories about themselves as well. They illustrated their religions — with pictures of their myths and their gods — and their economy — with pictures of the animals they hunted or depended on. We learn about what clothes people wore in earlier times by what their weaving was made into, and what materials were available to them by what the weaving was made of. Often we even learn the sex and social status of the weaver. (In some cultures weaving is done only by women, while in others it's done only by men!)

Try designing a weaving that tells a story about you and your life. Imagine someone finding it 1000 years from now. What would they discover about you? Remember, your weaving should be functional, too. It should warm you or protect you . . . (What other functions can woven material serve? Take a look around you to get some ideas.) Research weaving from other parts of the world and other ages to see what it tells us about other people and times. You might start with the Unicorn Tapestries of the Middle Ages, or Navajo Indian blankets (both old and new), or ancient weavings from Peru.

TRY DIFFERENT KINDS OF WEAVES

Over 1 Under 1
Over 1 Under 1
(called "tabby" weave)

Over 2 Under 2
Over 2 Under 2

Leave some warp
showing

Wrap yarn around several
warp strings

Weave in other materials:
grasses, leaves, tree bark,
cotton puffs, buttons,
small metal parts

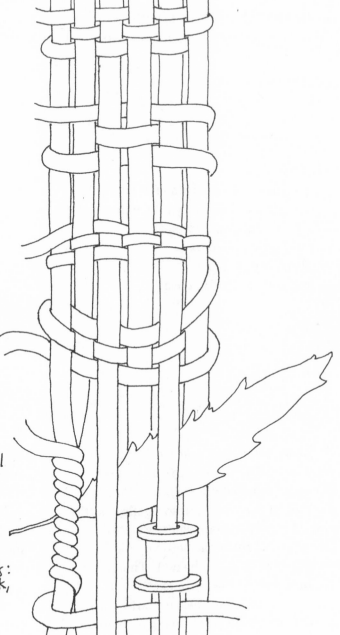

FABRIC DESIGN

Do this at a big empty table with all your supplies at one end and room for you to work at the other. Cover the table with newspaper and yourself with an apron.

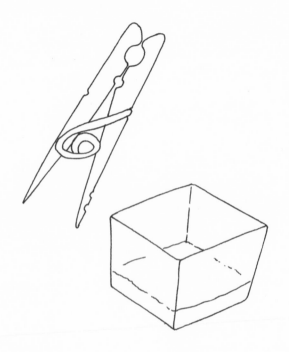

YOU NEED:
several plastic buckets (one for each color
    dye, one for bleach (if you're using
    bleach), and one for water
pinch-type clothespins
plenty of newspaper
an iron (set for medium heat)

DYE

If you are using light-colored fabric you will want to work with dye. Use an instant packaged dye like Rit or Tintex. Pour a package of dye powder into a gallon bottle and fill it with hot tap water. Put the cover on and shake the bottle up (be careful — it's hot and heavy). Then pour the liquid into a plastic bucket. Let it cool before you use it. It's best to start with 1 or 2 colors until you get the hang of dyeing.

BLEACH

If you are using dark-colored fabric you can use undiluted bleach to make designs. Where the bleach touches the fabric it takes out the color. Pour bleach into a plastic bucket until it is about 2″ deep. Do this near an open window so the smell isn't overpowering, and try not to touch the bleach or smell it directly. Always use a clothespin for putting your fabric in and taking it out, and be sure to rinse the fabric in water immediately.

Tie Dye

TIE DYE and BATIK are both called "resist processes" because in certain places the fabric resists (or doesn't take in) the dye.

1. Tie rubber bands or string as tightly as you can around your fabric in several places.

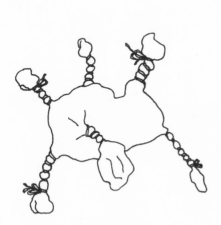

Try different ways of tying

2. Place the fabric in the dye or bleach for 2 to 3 minutes. Different fabrics take different lengths of time to dye or bleach. Your fabric is "done" when it's a little darker than you want it to be if you're dyeing it, or when it's just as light as you want it to be if you're bleaching it.

3. Pick it up with a clothespin and swish it in the bucket of water for a minute. (Some of the dye or bleach will come out in the water. You will have to change the water from time to time.)

4. Wrap it up in a piece of newspaper and press some of the water out.

5. Take out the ties and hang the fabric up to dry (or iron it dry)

or

leave the ties in, tie in some new ones, and put the fabric into a new color dye.

Batik

YOU NEED:

a stove or hot plate (set for low heat)
a saucepan or large tin can
a smaller tin can
cheap paint brushes (which will become
    permanent wax brushes)
paraffin (Paraffin is sold in 1-pound boxes
    in hardware stores. 1 box will be
    enough for several projects.)

1. Fill the saucepan or large tin can halfway with water and put it on the stove or hot plate.

2. Put some paraffin in the small tin can and put this can in the can of water.

3. When the paraffin is melted, paint a picture or design with it on your fabric. Use a lot of wax to be sure it penetrates the fabric. You can paint the back of the fabric also to be extra sure.

4. Put the fabric into the bleach or the dye for 2 to 3 minutes.

5. Take it out with a clothespin and swish it in the water.

6. Sandwich it between 4 sheets of newspaper (2 on top, 2 underneath) and iron it. When you see that the newspaper is full of wax, use fresh newspaper. When no more wax is being absorbed by the paper your batik is finished.

7. To do a 2 or more color batik, leave the wax in after each dyeing. Let the fabric dry. Then paint on more wax and re-dye. Do light colors first, then darker ones. After the last dye, iron out the wax.

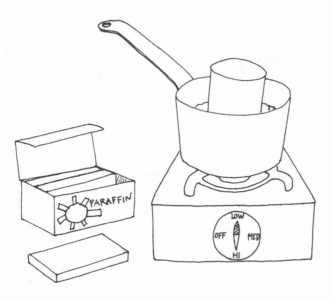

Printing & Painting on Fabric

Bleach and dye can be painted right onto fabric with a brush, or a sponge, or even a twig. Use undiluted bleach and BE PATIENT! It's like invisible writing — you can't see the results at first. It takes a few minutes for the bleach to work. Or use concentrated dye (mix 1 teaspoonful of dye powder in a cup of hot water) and paint with that.

To print an object on your fabric, dip it in BLEACH and press it onto the cloth. Try vegetables, sponges cut into interesting shapes, or other objects. LEAVES WORK REALLY WELL: dip a leaf in bleach and put it on the fabric. (Try not to drip the bleach.) Put 2 sheets of newspaper down on top. Rub the newspaper gently but firmly with your hand. Rinse the fabric in water to remove the excess bleach.

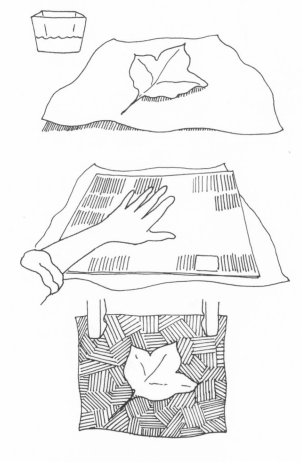

Crayon Batik

You can also use crayons to decorate fabric. Draw on the fabric the same way you would on paper. Then put it under a sheet of newspaper and iron it. The newspaper will absorb the wax from the crayons (you'll see your picture come off on the paper) but the pigment (the coloring in the crayon) will stay in the fabric. Each time you see your picture come off on the newspaper it's time to use a new sheet. When it stops coming off your fabric is finished.

This is a quick way to make T-shirts, but they'll fade when washed so you'll have to touch them up from time to time.

WHEELS

These are materials you might use to make cars, trucks, trains, and other wheeled vehicles. On the next pages are three ways of assembling the bodies, wheels and axles to make fast-rolling, free-wheeling toys.

FOR BODIES USE:

cigar boxes
milk cartons
orange juice cans
hairbrushes
oatmeal boxes
ice cream containers
scrap wood
shoeboxes
carpet tubes
milk crates
egg cartons
anything else you can possibly figure out
   how to put an axle on

FOR WHEELS USE:

ice cream lids
bottle caps and lids
wood beads
cardboard circles, cut from sturdy boxes
jar lids
milk bottle tops
ends of paper rolls from copier machines
   (ask at the library)
gears
buttons
thread spools
can lids with the edges filed
keep "wheels" in the back of your mind
   for the next 3 days and you'll come up
   with an assortment of useful ideas!

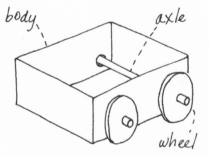

FOR AXLES USE:

dowels
pencils
2 plastic straws, one stuffed inside
   the other
paper logs (see CONSTRUCTIONS)
knitting needles
crochet hooks
toothpicks
lollipop sticks
wire coat hangers cut into pieces with a
   wire cutter

Model I

To make the cars on this page, the axles are glued to the body of the car and don't turn. The wheels are not glued to the axles and they do turn.

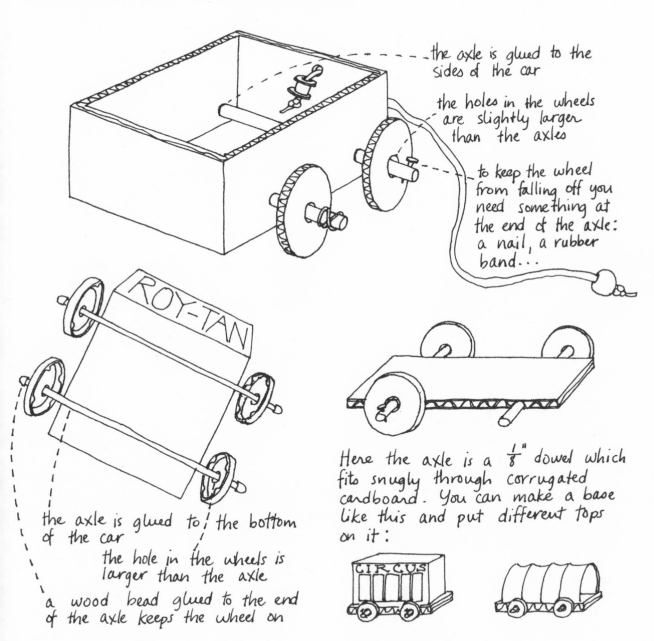

the axle is glued to the sides of the car

the holes in the wheels are slightly larger than the axles

to keep the wheel from falling off you need something at the end of the axle: a nail, a rubber band...

the axle is glued to the bottom of the car

the hole in the wheels is larger than the axle

a wood bead glued to the end of the axle keeps the wheel on

ROY-TAN

Here the axle is a $\frac{1}{8}''$ dowel which fits snugly through corrugated cardboard. You can make a base like this and put different tops on it:

CIRCUS

Model II

To make the cars on this page, the axles are not glued to the body of the car. They turn freely. The wheels are glued to the axles so they turn with them.

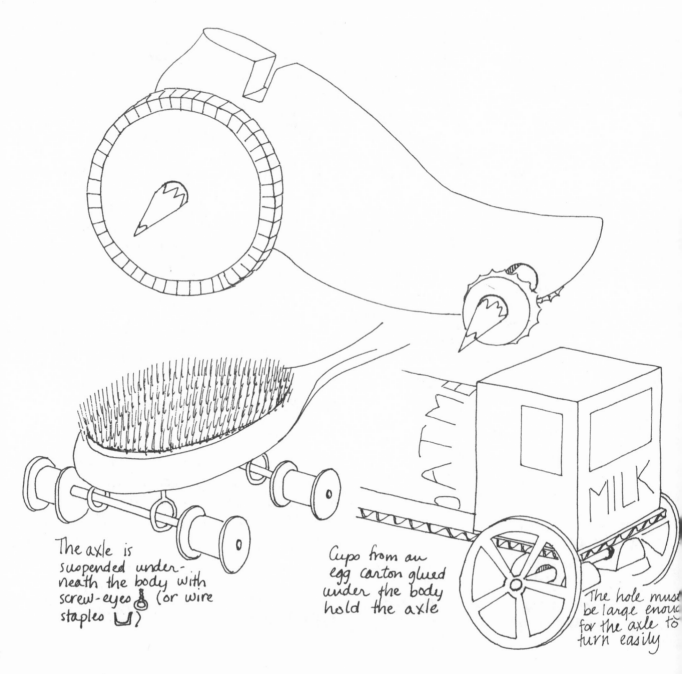

The axle is suspended underneath the body with screw-eyes ✦ (or wire staples ⊔)

Cups from an egg carton glued under the body hold the axle

The hole must be large enough for the axle to turn easily

Model III

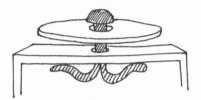

Here the wheels are attached with paper fasteners. They must be attached loosely with a little bit of space between the car body and the wheel. The hole in the wheel should be a little larger than the stem of the paper fastener so the wheel spins freely.

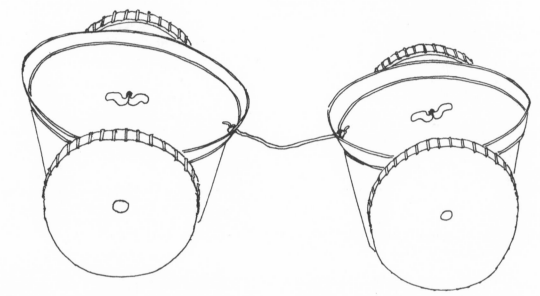

TO FASTEN CARS TOGETHER USE:

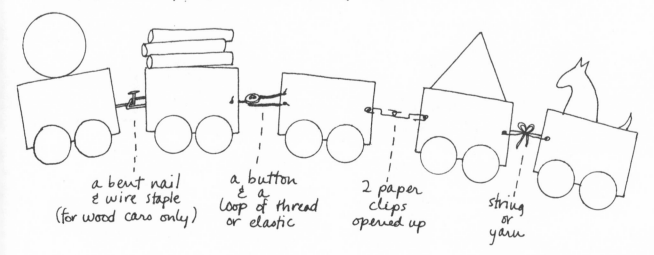

a bent nail & wire staple (for wood cars only)

a button & a loop of thread or elastic

2 paper clips opened up

string or yarn

DOLLS

Stuffed Doll

YOU NEED:

    2 pieces of fabric (for front and back of doll)
    a needle and thread
    straight pins
    stuffing (fabric scraps, old socks or stockings, yarn, or foam)
    a pencil
    scissors

1. Draw the shape of your doll on a piece of fabric.

2. Draw a line around the outside 1″ away from your outline.

3. Pin the 2 pieces of fabric to each other, right sides together. Make sure they're smooth and flat against each other.

4. Carefully cut along the outside line.

5. Sew all around the doll along the inside line using a backstitch.

   Leave a 2½″ opening on top of the head so you'll be able to stuff it.

6. Turn the doll inside out and push the stuffing in. Be sure to get it in all the corners.

7. Sew up the head with an overstitch.

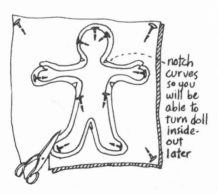

notch curves so you will be able to turn doll inside-out later

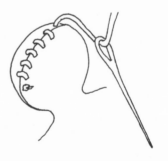

8. HAIR: Thread a needle with yarn 2' long (or longer if you want long hair). Sew into the head and out, leaving a 2" to 3" end. Make loops all over top and back of head. Use as many pieces of yarn as are necessary. To end yarn, tie end onto last loop.

Leave loops for curly hair or cut them for straight hair.

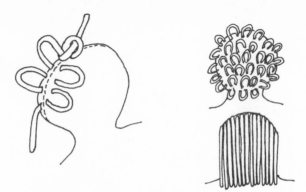

9. Sew on buttons or glue on fabric scraps to make a face.

Make a bean bag doll the same way. Fill it with dried peas or beans, uncooked rice, or small buttons.

QUICK STUFFED DOLL
  Sew 2 washcloths
    together.
  Stuff and decorate.

Dancing Doll

1. Out of lightweight cardboard cut:
   1 piece for the head and torso
   2 legs
   2 arms

2. Using a hole punch, punch 2 holes at the tops of the arms and legs and one hole at the shoulders and hips.

3. Fasten with string and paper fasteners as shown. Pull down on the string and the doll will dance.

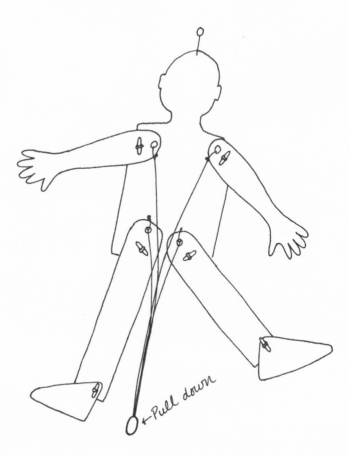

Pull down

Pipe Cleaner Doll

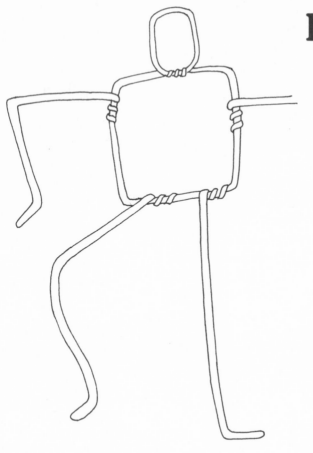

1. Twist pipe cleaners around each other to make a frame. You might use one for the head, one for the body, and one for each arm and leg.

2. Cut several strips of fabric about 1½" wide and wrap them around the frame to build the body up to the shape you want. (Stuff the torso with fabric to keep the doll from being too flat and wide.) Use a dab of glue at the end of each strip to keep it in place.

3. When the doll is the shape you want, dress it. Make a garment out of fabric by cutting out two identical pieces, a front and back. Sew them together; turn them inside out and put the garment on the doll.

make 2

Yarn Doll

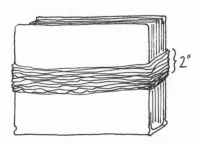

1. Rug yarn is best for this. Wrap yarn around a book until you have a strip 2" wide. Slip it off and cut one end.

2. Tie yarn together at uncut end.

3. Wad a piece of fabric into a ball about 2" in diameter and wrap the yarn around it. Tie it off underneath to form a head. Make the torso with another wad of fabric.

4. Tie off the torso. Braid the yarn below into 2 legs or leave it loose as a skirt.

5. To make arms, wrap more yarn around a shorter book until you have a strip 1" wide. Slip it off and cut both ends. Tie off one end and braid the rest. Tie the other end and slip the braid through the torso.

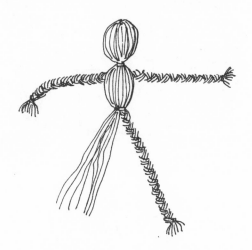

PUPPETS

FINGER PUPPETS

Cut a figure out of lightweight paper or cardboard. Leave tabs at the bottom with 2 holes for your fingers and "let your fingers do the walking."

OR

Leave tabs at bottom sides. Glue tabs into a circle so puppet will sit on your finger.

Fold

SPOON

GLOVES →

BLEACH BOTTLES

HAIRBRUSH

CLOTHES PINS

SOCK HOBBYHORSE

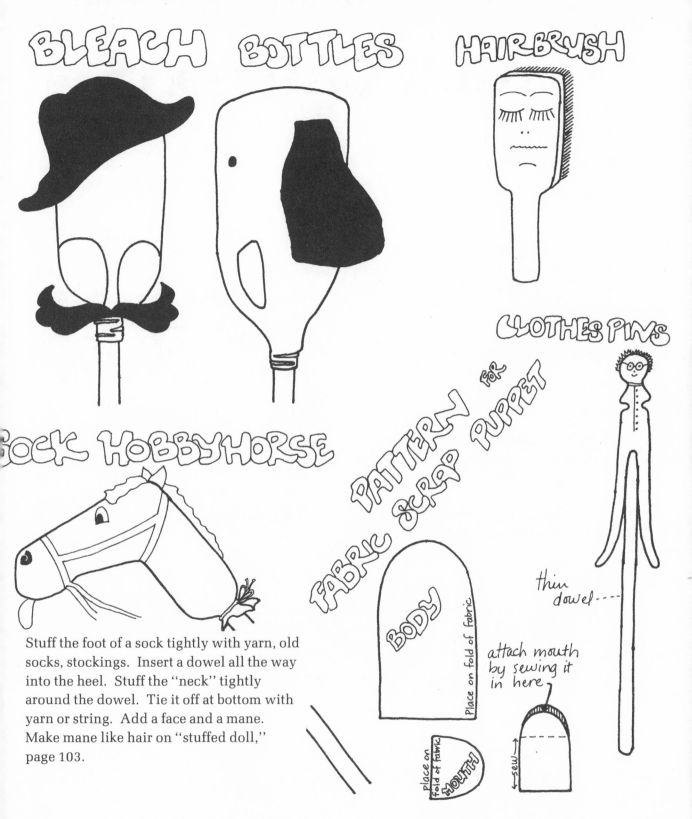

Stuff the foot of a sock tightly with yarn, old socks, stockings. Insert a dowel all the way into the heel. Stuff the "neck" tightly around the dowel. Tie it off at bottom with yarn or string. Add a face and a mane. Make mane like hair on "stuffed doll," page 103.

PATTERN for FABRIC SCRAP PUPPET

BODY

Place on fold of fabric

MOUTH

Place on fold of fabric

attach mouth by sewing it in here

sew

thin dowel

MILK CARTONS

USE THEM TO:

Make a model of your house or school

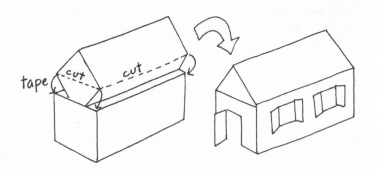  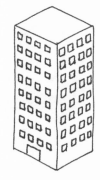

Map your neighborhood
  ½-pint cartons might be 1 story buildings
  quart cartons might be 2 to 3 story
      buildings
  ½-gallon cartons might be large public
      buildings (school, library, or town hall)

What's the ratio of 1 story buildings to
2 or 3 story ones? (How many 1's
compared to how many 2 or 3's?)

What's the ratio of empty space to built-
on space?

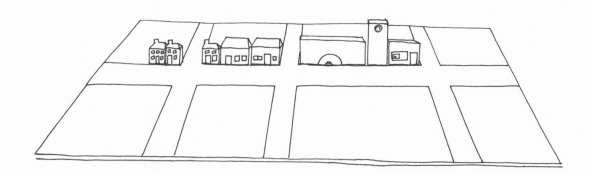

Puppet

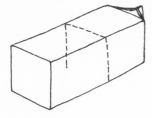

Slit 3 sides of a carton

Fold it back so that your hand fits inside. Glue on paper, fabric, or yarn to make a puppet head.

Boat

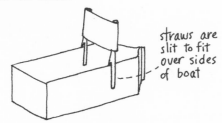

straws are slit to fit over sides of boat

Half a milk carton makes a natural boat. Rig up a sail with 2 straws and some paper, or

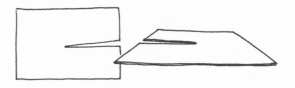

make a rubber band motor by slitting 2 small pieces of milk carton and fitting them together.

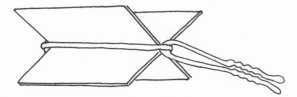

Slip a rubber band across the center and a hairpin at either end.

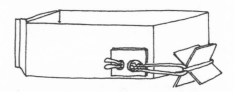

Attach the pins to the back of the boat by "pinning" them to another piece of milk carton glued to the sides. Glue them low so that the paddle wheel sits below the boat in the water and far enough back so that the wheel doesn't touch the boat.

TO USE: Put the boat in the water. Twist the wheel and let go.

What's the fastest boat you can make? Experiment with different types of sails, weights and rudders to see what controls the speed and direction of sail.

Water Dam

This is a good water-play or bathtub toy for preschoolers. Cut off one side of a milk carton. Out of that side cut a sliding gate and track. The gate raises and lowers to control the water flow. Seal the other end of the carton securely with staples and tape.

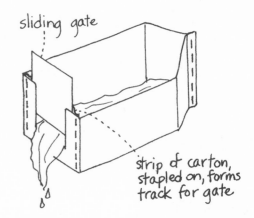

sliding gate

strip of carton, stapled on, forms track for gate

Film Strip

Draw scenes on a sheet of clear stiff acetate with a permanent marker. Pass the "film strip" through slits in the sides of a milk carton "viewer." In a dark room, shine a flashlight through the acetate against a blank wall. Pictures will project.

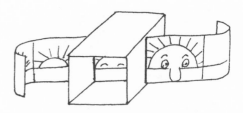

T.V.

Draw pictures with a permanent marker on clear acetate. Tape each end of the acetate to a pencil inside a milk carton viewer. Wind the acetate from one pencil to the other for viewing.

Printing Stencil

Cut off the sides of a milk carton. Cut shapes out of them, lay them on a piece of paper, and brush paint or ink through with a brush or sponge. Before the stencils dry, sandwich them between wax paper or plastic wrap and flatten under a heavy book. Then they can be reused.

Storage Unit

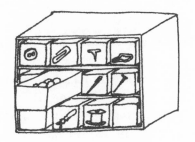

YOU NEED:

2 sturdy cardboard cartons with thick,
   rigid sides, one at least 4″ wider than
   the other
good scissors, glue, a ruler

1. Out of one carton cut shelves — as
   deep as the other carton and 4″ wider.

2. Measure off 2″ on either side and draw
   a line.

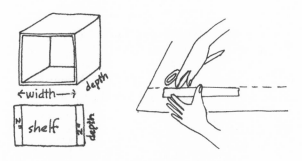

3. SCORE the lines by running one blade
   of a scissors along it. Hold the ruler
   there to help you make a straight line.
   The blade should mark the cardboard
   but not go all the way through.

4. Fold the 2″ tabs along the scored line.
   (The scoring should be on the outside
   of the fold.) Put glue along the tabs
   and fit the shelf into the other carton.

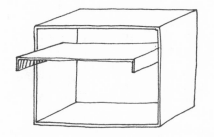

5. Rest milk cartons on the shelves to
   hold small objects.

Boxes

Cut away the sides of a milk carton to
leave a lid and tuck-in flaps. Decorate the
outside.

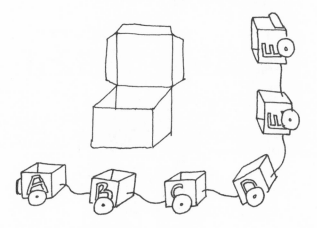

Terrarium

Use a ½-gallon or gallon carton. Cut out all 4 sides leaving a ½" frame all around. Cut 4 pieces of clear acetate the same size as each side of your carton and glue them to the inside of the carton.

Open the top to pour in soil. Make a hole in the soil with a wooden spoon and place plant in the hole.

Using the spoon, gently push soil around the plant and pack it down to hold the plant upright.

water lightly and seal the opening with masking tape (if mist forms open the top for a short while)

a layer of pebbles will allow for drainage

Planter

Cut a carton down to about 3" tall. Punch holes for strings. Glue yarn or paper to the outside to decorate.

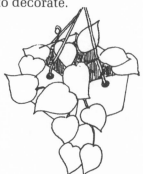

Slotted Card Construction

Cut the sides of a milk carton into squares, rectangles, triangles, circles and irregular shapes. Cut several ¼" deep slots in each. Use the cards to build structures.

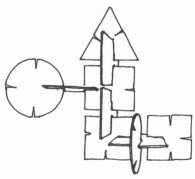

Make slotted cards (as above) and use them to build furniture
    for a doll house
    to make a model of your room, your house, your classroom. How might you rearrange it to make it fit your needs (or wants) better?
    to design your ideal house

Try working to scale: 1" = 1'. Measure the furniture and people around you and make your milk carton furniture in the same proportions. You'll discover some surprising things!

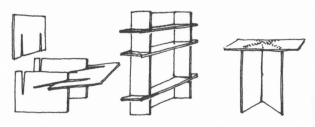

Milk Carton Balance

YOU NEED:

2 ½-gallon milk cartons
2 ½-pint milk cartons
sand (you can buy sand inexpensively at
   a hardware store)
a sheet of newspaper
a plastic dime-store ruler (the kind with a
   hole at each end and in the center)
a long nail and a hammer
string

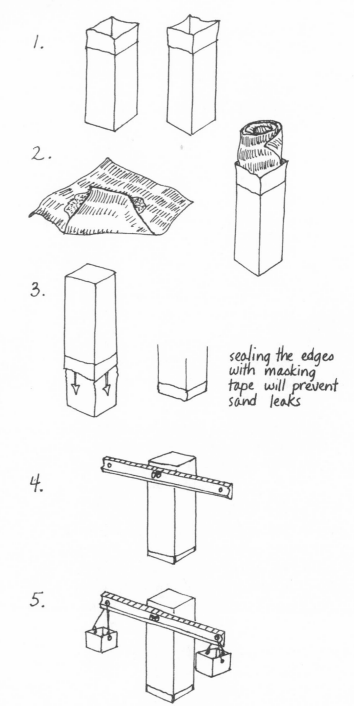

1. Open the tops of the ½-gallon cartons.

2. Pour several cupfuls of sand into the
   center of a sheet of newspaper and roll it
   up. Stuff the newspaper into one of the
   cartons.

3. Squeeze the other carton down over
   the one you stuffed. Push hard; try not
   to break the corners.

4. Use the ruler for the "beam." Hold it
   on by hammering the nail into the
   cartons 1″ from the top.

5. Cut the tops off the ½-pint cartons and
   punch holes in the sides to put string
   through. Attach them to the ruler,
   making sure they hang evenly about 4″
   high.

sealing the edges with masking tape will prevent sand leaks

Candle Making

Do this on a table covered with newspaper.

YOU NEED:
1 pound of paraffin, bought in a hardware
    store. This will make several small
    candles.
old crayons
a pencil
2 tin cans, one larger than the other
string
a stove or hot plate

1. Cut a milk carton down to the height
   you want your candle to be.

2. Wrap some string around a pencil and
   let it hang down in the center of the
   carton almost to the bottom. This will be
   the wick.

3. Fill half of the larger tin can with water
   and put it on the stove or hot plate set for
   low heat. Put a block of paraffin and a
   crayon (to color the candle) into the
   small can and put it in the can of water.

4. When the paraffin has melted turn the
   stove or hot plate off and carefully (it's
   very hot) pick up the small can with a
   potholder. SLOWLY pour the liquid
   paraffin into the milk carton, up to about
   1″ from the top.

5. Let it cool. When the paraffin is hard,
   peel the milk carton off.

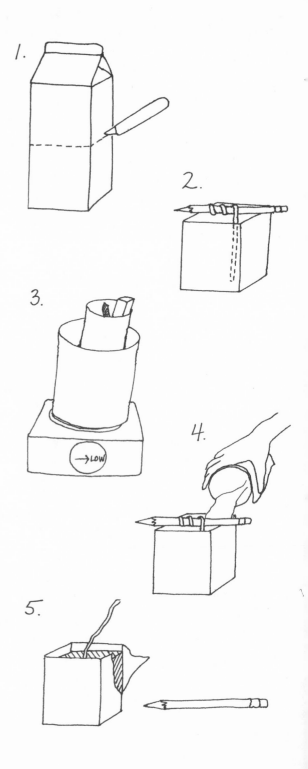

Carving

YOU NEED:

½-gallon or gallon milk cartons
plaster
carving tools (kitchen knife, chisel,
  screwdriver, nail, etc.)

1. Cut off one side of the milk carton.

2. Mix up the plaster according to the
   directions on the package and fill the
   milk carton with it.

3. When the plaster has hardened peel
   the carton away and use the tool(s) to
   to carve a form out of the plaster.

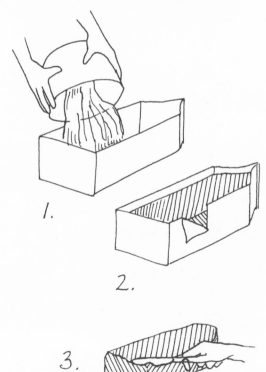

Sand Casting

YOU NEED:

damp sand
plaster
objects to cast
½-gallon or gallon milk cartons

1. Cut off one side of the milk carton.

2. Fill the milk carton with sand.

3. Press an object into the sand or scoop
   some of the sand out to make a mold.

4. Mix up the plaster according to the
   directions on the package and pour in
   just enough to fill the mold. Let it
   harden.

MATCHING GAME: Make casts of leaves
or hands or other objects. See if you can
match the casts up with the originals.

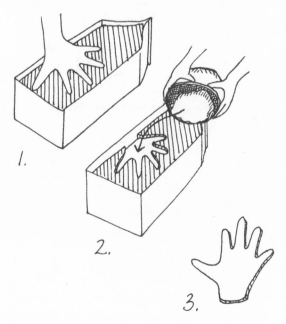

QUICKIES

Beads

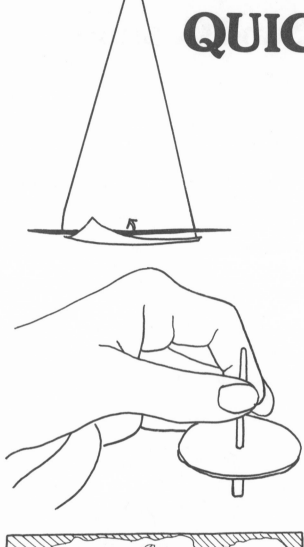

Cut a long skinny triangle out of glossy magazine paper or leather scraps. Roll it around a toothpick from base to point and fasten it at the end with a tiny dab of glue. Remove the toothpick and there's a hole for stringing. (Small children can do this on a pencil instead of a toothpick.)

They make beautiful necklaces!

Tops

Cut a circle out of cardboard about 2″ in diameter. Push a toothpick through the center and spin it.

Try different size circles. Try a pencil instead of a toothpick. Can you make a top that writes?

Can you control the length of spin? The distance it moves? The speed of spin?

Torn Paper Pictures

Tear shapes from colored paper, magazines or newspapers and paste them down to make pictures.

Good for little kids who can't cut — and big kids who think they can't draw.

Button Spinners

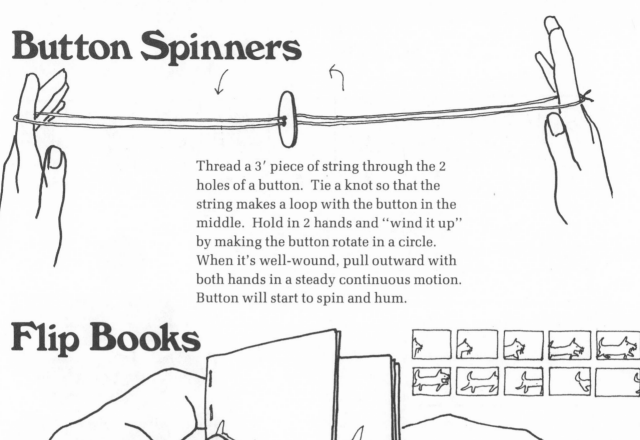

Thread a 3' piece of string through the 2 holes of a button. Tie a knot so that the string makes a loop with the button in the middle. Hold in 2 hands and "wind it up" by making the button rotate in a circle. When it's well-wound, pull outward with both hands in a steady continuous motion. Button will start to spin and hum.

Flip Books

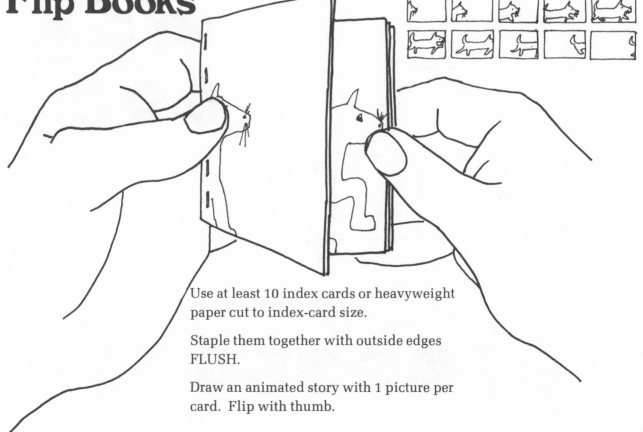

Use at least 10 index cards or heavyweight paper cut to index-card size.

Staple them together with outside edges FLUSH.

Draw an animated story with 1 picture per card. Flip with thumb.

SOLUTIONS TO PUZZLES

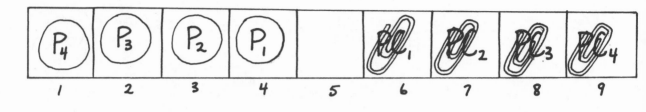

	1	2	3	4	5	6	7	8	9

1. P_1 to 5
2. PC_1 to 4
3. PC_2 to 6
4. P_1 to 7
5. P_2 to 5
6. P_3 to 3
7. PC_1 to 2
8. PC_2 to 4

9. PC_3 to 6
10. PC_4 to 8
11. P_1 to 9
12. P_2 to 7
13. P_3 to 5
14. P_4 to 3
15. PC_1 to 1
16. PC_2 to 2

17. PC_3 to 4
18. PC_4 to 6
19. P_2 to 8
20. P_3 to 7
21. P_4 to 5
22. PC_3 to 3
23. PC_4 to 4
24. P_4 to 6

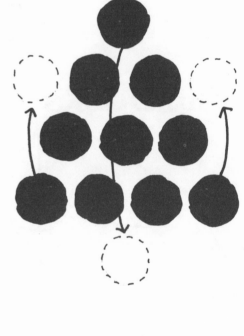

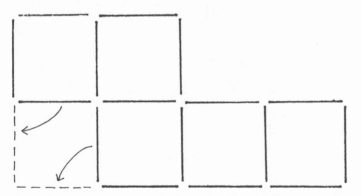

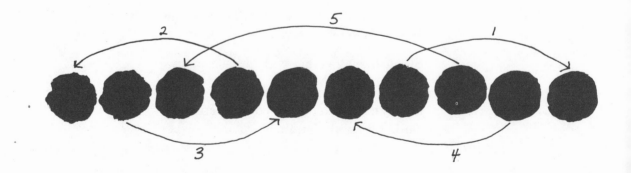